Hands-On Deep Learning with PyTorch

From Fundamentals to Advanced Projects

©
Written By
Camila Jones

Copyright Page

Hands-On Deep Learning with PyTorch: From Fundamentals to Advanced Projects
Copyright © 2025 by [Author's Name]
All rights reserved.

Disclaimer:
This book is designed to provide accurate and authoritative information regarding the subject matter covered. While every effort has been made to ensure the accuracy of the information presented, the author and publisher make no representations or warranties with respect to the accuracy, completeness, or applicability of the contents. The author and publisher disclaim any liability for any direct, indirect, incidental, or consequential damages arising from the use of this book.

Table of Content

Part 1

Introduction to Deep Learning and PyTorch

Chapter 1: Introduction to Deep Learning and PyTorch

This chapter serves as an introduction to **deep learning** and **PyTorch**, a powerful framework that allows us to implement deep learning models. It will provide the foundational understanding needed to proceed with more advanced topics and practical applications. By the end of this chapter, you will have a solid understanding of what deep learning is, why PyTorch is a preferred framework, and how to set up the environment for your work.

1.1. What is Deep Learning?

Deep learning is a subset of **machine learning**, which is itself a part of **artificial intelligence (AI)**. At a high level, deep learning involves training algorithms known as **neural networks** to automatically learn patterns in data. These patterns can be simple, like detecting shapes in images, or complex, like translating text from one language to another.

Key Concepts:

- **Neural Networks**: The backbone of deep learning, these are composed of layers of interconnected nodes (also called neurons) that process information. Neural networks are inspired by the human brain's structure, with layers that transform data progressively to identify patterns or make predictions.

- **Learning from Data**: In deep learning, the model automatically improves as it is exposed to more data. This is done through the **training** process, where the model makes predictions, compares them to the actual outcomes (called **labels**), and adjusts itself accordingly using a process called

backpropagation.

- **Deep Networks**: The term **"deep"** in deep learning refers to the use of many layers (often hundreds or thousands) in a neural network. More layers allow the model to learn complex representations, making deep learning particularly powerful for tasks like image recognition, natural language processing, and speech recognition.

Why is Deep Learning Important?

Deep learning has enabled breakthroughs in many industries. For example:

- **Image Recognition**: Deep learning has allowed machines to identify objects in images and videos at or above human-level performance.
- **Natural Language Processing (NLP)**: Deep learning has revolutionized tasks like language translation, sentiment analysis, and speech recognition.
- **Healthcare**: Deep learning models are used in medical imaging, diagnostics, and drug discovery, saving lives and improving healthcare efficiency.

Deep learning models excel at handling **large-scale data** and can automatically learn the **features** that are crucial for solving complex problems. This ability to learn without manual feature extraction sets deep learning apart from traditional machine learning techniques.

1.2. History and Evolution of Deep Learning

The evolution of deep learning has been shaped by several key milestones in computing and mathematics. Understanding this evolution provides valuable context for appreciating the significance of current advancements.

Early Beginnings (1940s-1980s):

- **1943**: The concept of artificial neurons was introduced by **Warren McCulloch** and **Walter Pitts**, who modeled neurons in the brain as simple logic gates.
- **1958**: **Frank Rosenblatt** invented the **perceptron**, the first neural network that could learn by adjusting weights, laying the groundwork for later neural network architectures.

Rise and Fall of Neural Networks (1980s-2000s):

- **1986**: The **backpropagation** algorithm was introduced by **Geoffrey Hinton**, **David Rumelhart**, and **Ronald Williams**. This method allowed neural networks to be trained efficiently, leading to a resurgence of interest in neural networks.
- Despite these advancements, computing power and data limitations led to a decline in neural network research throughout the 1990s, with alternatives like **support vector machines (SVMs)** gaining more traction.

Breakthroughs and Modern Deep Learning (2006-Present):

- **2006**: **Geoffrey Hinton** and colleagues introduced the concept of **deep belief networks**, marking the beginning of modern deep learning.
- **2012**: The turning point came when **AlexNet**, a deep convolutional neural network (CNN) developed by **Alex Krizhevsky**, won the **ImageNet Large Scale Visual Recognition Challenge** (ILSVRC) by a wide margin, demonstrating the power of deep learning for image recognition.
- Since 2012, deep learning has seen rapid advancements, with **convolutional neural networks (CNNs)** becoming the go-to model for image-related tasks, and **transformers** revolutionizing natural language processing.

1.3. Key Applications of Deep Learning

Deep learning has been successfully applied in a wide range of fields, delivering state-of-the-art performance in many tasks.

Deep learning models, particularly CNNs, have made tremendous strides in tasks such as:

- **Object Detection**: Identifying and locating objects in images (e.g., faces, cars).
- **Image Classification**: Categorizing images into classes (e.g., "cat," "dog").
- **Image Generation**: Creating realistic images using models like **Generative Adversarial Networks (GANs)**.

Deep learning models like **transformers** have enabled:

- **Machine Translation**: Translating text between languages (e.g., Google Translate).
- **Sentiment Analysis**: Understanding the sentiment in text (e.g., reviews, social media).
- **Text Generation**: Generating coherent and contextually relevant text (e.g., GPT-3).
- **Deep learning models** have made significant improvements in converting spoken language into text, enabling virtual assistants like **Siri** and **Alexa**.
- **Medical Imaging**: Deep learning is used for detecting diseases like cancer in X-rays, MRIs, and CT scans.
- **Drug Discovery**: Accelerating the process of finding new medications by predicting molecular interactions.

1.4. Why PyTorch?

PyTorch is an open-source deep learning framework that has become one of the most widely used tools for developing deep learning models. Here are the reasons why PyTorch stands out:

Unlike other frameworks that use static computation graphs, PyTorch uses **dynamic computation graphs** (also called **define-by-run**), meaning the graph is built at runtime. This provides greater flexibility for debugging and building complex models, as you can inspect and modify the graph on the fly.

PyTorch's API is clean and intuitive. It is designed to feel like Python, making it accessible to both researchers and developers. The framework is highly modular, allowing users to easily build, test, and optimize their models.

PyTorch has become the framework of choice for research and academia due to its simplicity and flexibility. It has a strong community, contributing to an ever-growing ecosystem of tools, tutorials, and resources.

PyTorch integrates seamlessly with CUDA, NVIDIA's parallel computing platform, to enable GPU acceleration. This makes it easier to train models on large datasets, which is a necessity for deep learning.

TorchScript allows you to serialize and optimize PyTorch models for deployment in production environments, making it easy to deploy models on mobile devices, edge devices, or server-side applications.

1.5. PyTorch vs. Other Deep Learning Frameworks

While there are other popular deep learning frameworks like **TensorFlow** and **Keras**, PyTorch has its unique advantages.

Feature	PyTorch	TensorFlow
Computation Graph	Dynamic (define-by-run)	Static (define-before-run)

Debugging	Easier (Pythonic, debug like Python)	Harder (requires TensorFlow debugging tools)
Learning Curve	Low (intuitive and easy to learn)	Steep (more complex, especially for beginners)
Deployment	Supports production (TorchScript)	Wide support in production (TensorFlow Lite, TensorFlow Serving)
Community and Support	Strong (research community)	Strong (industry support)

Advantages of PyTorch:

- **Dynamic computation graph** is more flexible, making it easier to work with complex models and debug them.
- **Pythonic syntax** makes it more intuitive for Python developers.
- **Faster prototyping**, enabling researchers to test new ideas more quickly.

1.6. Setting Up the PyTorch Environment

Before you can start building deep learning models, you need to set up your PyTorch environment. This involves installing Python, PyTorch, and some additional dependencies for optimal performance.

To install PyTorch, you first need to ensure that you have **Python 3.x** installed. You can download it from the official Python website (python.org).

To install PyTorch, you can use pip, Python's package installer.

pip install torch torchvision

Alternatively, you can use **Conda**, a package manager that handles dependencies and environment management more efficiently, especially for scientific computing.

conda install pytorch torchvision torchaudio cudatoolkit=11.0 -c pytorch

This installs PyTorch along with the required libraries.

It's recommended to use **Conda** environments to avoid conflicts with other Python packages. You can create a new environment by running:

conda create -n pytorch_env python=3.8
conda activate pytorch_env

Then, install PyTorch as shown above.

To verify that PyTorch is correctly installed, you can run a quick test in Python:

import torch
print(torch.__version__)
print(torch.cuda.is_available()) # Checks if CUDA (GPU support) is enabled

If this runs without errors, then PyTorch has been successfully installed.

1.7. Overview of the Book Structure

This book is structured to take you on a journey from learning the basic principles of deep learning to building and deploying advanced models.

- **Part 1** introduces deep learning, PyTorch, and how to set up the environment.
- **Part 2** covers building neural networks, regularization techniques, and advanced training strategies.
- **Part 3** dives into intermediate topics such as CNNs, RNNs, transformers, and generative models.
- **Part 4** explores advanced topics like reinforcement learning and model deployment.
- **Part 5** presents hands-on practical projects, applying what you've learned to real-world tasks.
- **Part 6** includes appendices with best practices, troubleshooting tips, and further learning resources.

By the end of this book, you'll have a deep understanding of PyTorch and deep learning, and you'll be able to build, optimize, and deploy your own models.

This chapter has laid the groundwork for your deep learning journey. You now have a basic understanding of deep learning, its history, key applications, and why PyTorch is an excellent choice for implementing your models. Next, we'll dive into the core PyTorch concepts in **Chapter 2**, where we'll begin hands-on exploration of tensors and neural networks.

Chapter 2: Basic PyTorch Concepts

In this chapter, we will explore the fundamental concepts that form the backbone of working with deep learning in PyTorch. These concepts include **tensors**, **automatic differentiation**, **nn.Module**, **GPU acceleration**, and **data handling**. Understanding these foundational concepts will enable you to build efficient and effective deep learning models in PyTorch.

2.1. Introduction to Tensors

Tensors are the core data structure in PyTorch, akin to NumPy arrays, but with the added benefit of being able to operate on **GPUs** for faster computation. A tensor can represent scalar values, vectors, matrices, or higher-dimensional data.

Tensors in PyTorch can be created in several ways, and you can customize their shape, data type, and values.

- **From Python Lists**: You can create a tensor from a Python list using torch.tensor.

python
Copy code
```
import torch

# Create a tensor from a list
tensor_from_list = torch.tensor([1.0, 2.0, 3.0, 4.0])
print(tensor_from_list)
```

- **From NumPy Arrays**: PyTorch seamlessly integrates with NumPy, and you can convert a NumPy array into a tensor.

python

Copy code

```python
import numpy as np

numpy_array = np.array([1, 2, 3, 4])
tensor_from_numpy = torch.from_numpy(numpy_array)
print(tensor_from_numpy)
```

- **With Specific Values**: PyTorch provides functions to create tensors filled with specific values:
  - **Zeros**: Create a tensor filled with zeros.

python

Copy code

```python
zeros_tensor = torch.zeros(3, 3)  # 3x3 tensor of zeros
print(zeros_tensor)
```

- **Ones**: Create a tensor filled with ones.

python

Copy code

```python
ones_tensor = torch.ones(2, 4)  # 2x4 tensor of ones
print(ones_tensor)
```

- **Random Values**: Create a tensor with values randomly sampled from a uniform distribution between 0 and 1.

python

Copy code

```python
random_tensor = torch.rand(2, 3)  # 2x3 tensor of random values
```

```
print(random_tensor)
```

- **Uninitialized Tensor**: Create an uninitialized tensor (values may be random).

python

Copy code

```
uninitialized_tensor = torch.empty(3, 2)  # 3x2 uninitialized tensor
print(uninitialized_tensor)
```

Once tensors are created, you can perform numerous operations on them. These operations are similar to those in NumPy but include some additional features to make them more efficient for deep learning tasks.

- **Element-wise Operations**: You can perform arithmetic operations on tensors element by element.

python

Copy code

```
tensor_a = torch.tensor([1, 2, 3])
tensor_b = torch.tensor([4, 5, 6])

sum_tensor = tensor_a + tensor_b  # Element-wise addition
print(sum_tensor)
```

- **Matrix Multiplication**: For matrix multiplication, PyTorch provides the torch.mm() function. You can also use the @ operator.

python

Copy code

```python
tensor_a = torch.tensor([[1, 2], [3, 4]])
tensor_b = torch.tensor([[5, 6], [7, 8]])

product_tensor = torch.mm(tensor_a, tensor_b)  # Matrix multiplication
print(product_tensor)
```

- **In-place Operations**: In-place operations modify a tensor directly and are denoted by an underscore (_), which avoids memory overhead.

python

Copy code

```python
tensor_a.add_(2)  # In-place addition
print(tensor_a)
```

- **Element-wise Operations**: Operations like addition, subtraction, multiplication, and division work element-wise across tensors.

python

Copy code

```python
tensor_a = torch.tensor([1, 2, 3])
element_wise_add = tensor_a + 2  # Add 2 to each element
print(element_wise_add)
```

Broadcasting is a powerful feature that allows PyTorch to perform operations on tensors of different shapes without requiring explicit expansion. It automatically expands the smaller tensor to match the shape of the larger one.

For example, adding a scalar to a tensor is automatically broadcasted:

python

Copy code

```
tensor_a = torch.tensor([1, 2, 3])
tensor_b = torch.tensor([[1], [2], [3]])


broadcasted_result = tensor_a + tensor_b  # Broadcasting
print(broadcasted_result)
```

Here, tensor_a (a 1D tensor) is broadcasted to match the shape of tensor_b (a 2D tensor), allowing the operation to proceed element-wise.

2.2. Autograd and Automatic Differentiation

Autograd is the automatic differentiation system in PyTorch. It allows you to compute the gradients of tensors, which is essential for training neural networks.

Autograd automatically records the operations on tensors that have the requires_grad=True flag. It then builds a **computation graph** for the operations, allowing PyTorch to calculate gradients during backpropagation.

python

Copy code

```
# Create a tensor with gradient tracking
x = torch.tensor([2.0, 3.0], requires_grad=True)
y = x * x  # Apply an operation on x
```

```python
z = y.mean()  # Take the mean of y


z.backward()  # Compute gradients
print(x.grad)  # Print gradients with respect to x
```

In this example, the gradients of z with respect to x are computed using the chain rule. Autograd allows this computation to be done automatically.

You can access the gradients of any tensor using .grad. Here's a basic example using torch.autograd:

python

Copy code

```python
# Create a tensor that requires gradients
x = torch.tensor([2.0, 3.0], requires_grad=True)


# Perform a simple operation
y = x * 2


# Compute the gradients
y.backward()


# Print the gradient of x
print(x.grad)  # Output will be tensor([2., 2.])
```

The .backward() function computes the derivatives (gradients) of the tensor y with respect to x. PyTorch computes the gradients automatically using the chain rule.

In deep learning, the process of **backpropagation** allows us to compute the gradients of the loss function with respect to the model parameters. Here's an example of how PyTorch computes gradients in a simple neural network:

python
Copy code

```python
import torch
import torch.nn as nn

# Define a simple neural network
model = nn.Linear(2, 1)

# Input tensor
input_tensor = torch.tensor([[1.0, 2.0]])

# Output prediction
output = model(input_tensor)

# Define a target and compute the loss
target = torch.tensor([[1.0]])
loss = nn.MSELoss()(output, target)

# Compute gradients
loss.backward()

# Print the gradients
print(model.weight.grad)  # Gradients of the weights
print(model.bias.grad)  # Gradients of the bias
```

Here, after computing the loss, the .backward() function computes the gradients of the loss with respect to the weights and biases of the model.

2.3. PyTorch nn.Module

The nn.Module class is the base class for all neural network models in PyTorch. It provides a structured way to define your model, including the layers and how data passes through them during the forward pass.

All PyTorch models inherit from nn.Module. This allows you to organize your model's layers, weights, and forward pass in a consistent manner. The __init__ method defines the layers, and the forward method defines how data flows through these layers.

Let's build a simple neural network using nn.Module to demonstrate how to define layers and a forward pass.

python
Copy code

```python
import torch
import torch.nn as nn


# Define a simple fully connected neural network
class SimpleNN(nn.Module):
    def __init__(self):
        super(SimpleNN, self).__init__()
        self.fc1 = nn.Linear(2, 4)  # Input layer to hidden layer
        self.fc2 = nn.Linear(4, 1)  # Hidden layer to output layer

    def forward(self, x):
        x = torch.relu(self.fc1(x))  # Apply ReLU activation
```

```
    x = self.fc2(x)  # Output layer
    return x

# Instantiate the model
model = SimpleNN()

# Create a sample input
input_tensor = torch.tensor([[1.0, 2.0]])

# Pass the input through the model
output = model(input_tensor)
print(output)
```

In this example, we define a neural network with one hidden layer, apply a ReLU activation function, and output a single value.

2.4. GPU Acceleration with CUDA

Using **GPU acceleration** can significantly speed up the training of deep learning models. PyTorch supports **CUDA**, NVIDIA's parallel computing platform, to move tensor operations from the CPU to the GPU.

GPUs are designed to perform many calculations simultaneously, making them highly efficient for deep learning tasks that require significant computational resources. By leveraging CUDA, PyTorch can offload tensor operations to the GPU, significantly speeding up training times, especially for large models and datasets.

To use the GPU, you first need to check if a CUDA-enabled device is available. If so, you can move tensors to the GPU using the .to() method or .cuda().

python

Copy code

```python
device = torch.device("cuda" if torch.cuda.is_available() else "cpu")

# Create a tensor
tensor = torch.randn(3, 3)

# Move tensor to GPU if available
tensor = tensor.to(device)
print(tensor)
```

While using the GPU can speed up computations, it's important to keep an eye on memory usage. Using larger models and datasets may cause memory overflow. Here are a few tips for better performance:

- Use **batch processing** to divide data into smaller chunks.
- Optimize the model's **architecture** to reduce the number of parameters.
- Use **mixed precision training** to reduce memory usage and improve speed.

2.5. PyTorch Data Handling

Efficient data handling is essential for training deep learning models. PyTorch provides the torch.utils.data module, which makes it easy to load, process, and manage large datasets.

The torch.utils.data module contains two key classes: Dataset and DataLoader. Dataset is an abstract class that allows you to access individual data samples, while DataLoader provides utilities for batching, shuffling, and loading the data in parallel.

You can create a custom dataset by subclassing the Dataset class and overriding the __len__ and __getitem__ methods.

python

Copy code

```python
from torch.utils.data import Dataset

class CustomDataset(Dataset):
    def __init__(self, data, labels):
        self.data = data
        self.labels = labels

    def __len__(self):
        return len(self.data)

    def __getitem__(self, index):
        return self.data[index], self.labels[index]
```

Once you have defined your dataset, you can use DataLoader to manage batching, shuffling, and parallel loading of data:

python

Copy code

```python
from torch.utils.data import DataLoader

# Create a DataLoader for our custom dataset
dataset = CustomDataset(data=torch.randn(100, 10),
labels=torch.randn(100, 1))
dataloader = DataLoader(dataset, batch_size=10,
shuffle=True)
```

```
# Iterate through the DataLoader
for data, labels in dataloader:
    print(data.shape, labels.shape)
```

The DataLoader automatically handles batching and shuffling, making it easier to work with large datasets during training.

In this chapter, we've covered the essential concepts that form the foundation of deep learning with PyTorch. You now understand how to work with **tensors**, perform **autograd** for backpropagation, define models using **nn.Module**, leverage **GPU acceleration**, and handle **data** effectively. These concepts will be crucial as you move forward to building and training more complex deep learning models in the upcoming chapters.

Part 2

Neural Networks and Training Techniques

Chapter 3: Building Neural Networks with PyTorch

This chapter will guide you through the process of building neural networks in PyTorch. We'll start by discussing **layers**and **activation functions**, then move on to **loss functions** and **optimizers**, and finally explore **backpropagation** and **training loops**. By the end of this chapter, you'll be able to build, train, and optimize neural networks.

3.1. Layers and Activation Functions

In deep learning, a neural network is composed of layers that transform input data into meaningful output. Each layer performs a specific task such as computing weighted sums of inputs or applying activation functions.

The most basic type of layer in a neural network is the **fully connected layer**, or **dense layer**. In PyTorch, you can implement fully connected layers using the nn.Linear class.

A fully connected layer takes an input vector and computes a weighted sum, followed by a bias term. The equation for this operation is:

output=W·X+boutput=W·X+b

Where:

- $W$$W$ is the weight matrix,
- $X$$X$ is the input vector,
- $b$$b$ is the bias vector.

Creating a Fully Connected Layer:

python
Copy code

```
import torch
import torch.nn as nn

# Define a simple fully connected layer
fc_layer = nn.Linear(in_features=3, out_features=2)

# Create a sample input tensor
input_tensor = torch.tensor([[1.0, 2.0, 3.0]])

# Pass input through the fully connected layer
output = fc_layer(input_tensor)
print(output)
```

In this example:

- in_features=3: The layer expects 3 input features.
- out_features=2: The layer will output 2 values.

The nn.Linear class automatically initializes the weights WW and bias bb, which are adjusted during training.

Activation functions introduce non-linearity into the network, allowing it to learn complex patterns. Without activation functions, the network would just be performing a series of linear operations, making it equivalent to a linear regression model, no matter how many layers it has.

- **ReLU (Rectified Linear Unit)**: ReLU is one of the most commonly used activation functions. It outputs 0 for negative inputs and outputs the input itself for positive values.

$\text{ReLU}(x) = \max(0, x) \text{ReLU}(x) = \max(0, x)$

Using ReLU:

python

Copy code

```
relu = nn.ReLU()

# Sample input tensor
input_tensor = torch.tensor([[-1.0, 2.0, -3.0, 4.0]])

# Apply ReLU activation function
output_tensor = relu(input_tensor)
print(output_tensor)
```

- **Sigmoid**: The sigmoid function maps values to a range between 0 and 1. It's often used for binary classification problems.

$$\text{Sigmoid}(x) = \frac{1}{1+e-x} \text{Sigmoid}(x) = 1+e-x1$$

Using Sigmoid:

python

Copy code

```
sigmoid = nn.Sigmoid()

# Sample input tensor
input_tensor = torch.tensor([[-1.0, 2.0, 0.5]])

# Apply sigmoid activation function
output_tensor = sigmoid(input_tensor)
print(output_tensor)
```

- **Tanh (Hyperbolic Tangent)**: The tanh function is similar to the sigmoid, but its output range is between -1 and 1. It's commonly used in hidden layers of neural networks.

$$Tanh(x)=ex-e-xex+e-xTanh(x)=ex+e-xex-e-x$$

Using Tanh:

python
Copy code
```
tanh = nn.Tanh()

# Sample input tensor
input_tensor = torch.tensor([[-1.0, 2.0, 0.5]])

# Apply tanh activation function
output_tensor = tanh(input_tensor)
print(output_tensor)
```

You can also define your own custom activation functions in PyTorch. Here's an example of creating a simple **Leaky ReLU** activation function.

python
Copy code
```
class LeakyReLU(nn.Module):
    def __init__(self, negative_slope=0.01):
        super(LeakyReLU, self).__init__()
        self.negative_slope = negative_slope

    def forward(self, input):
```

```python
    return torch.where(input > 0, input, input * self.negative_slope)

# Instantiate the custom activation function
leaky_relu = LeakyReLU()

# Apply the custom activation
input_tensor = torch.tensor([[-1.0, 2.0, -0.5, 4.0]])
output_tensor = leaky_relu(input_tensor)
print(output_tensor)
```

This custom Leaky ReLU outputs a small negative value for negative inputs (scaled by the negative_slope parameter).

3.2. Loss Functions and Optimizers

Loss functions and optimizers are critical components of the training process. The **loss function** measures how far the model's predictions are from the true labels, while the **optimizer** adjusts the model's parameters to minimize the loss.

- **Mean Squared Error (MSE) Loss**: Used for regression tasks, MSE computes the squared difference between predicted and actual values.

python
Copy code
```python
mse_loss = nn.MSELoss()

# Sample target and prediction
target = torch.tensor([[1.0]])
```

```python
prediction = torch.tensor([[2.0]])

# Compute MSE loss
loss = mse_loss(prediction, target)
print(loss)
```

- **Cross-Entropy Loss**: Commonly used for classification tasks, especially multi-class classification. It measures the difference between two probability distributions (the true class distribution and the predicted distribution).

python

Copy code

```python
cross_entropy_loss = nn.CrossEntropyLoss()

# Sample target and prediction for multi-class classification
target = torch.tensor([1])  # Correct class index
prediction = torch.tensor([[1.5, 0.2, 0.3]])  # Model's raw output (logits)

# Compute Cross-Entropy loss
loss = cross_entropy_loss(prediction, target)
print(loss)
```

An **optimizer** updates the model's parameters (weights and biases) based on the gradients computed during backpropagation. The most common optimizer is **Stochastic Gradient Descent (SGD)**, but PyTorch also provides several other optimizers such as **Adam** and **RMSprop**.

- **Stochastic Gradient Descent (SGD)**: A basic optimization technique where parameters are updated by subtracting the gradient multiplied by the learning rate.

python

Copy code

```python
optimizer = torch.optim.SGD(model.parameters(), lr=0.01)

# Example: Updating weights using SGD
optimizer.zero_grad()  # Reset gradients to zero
loss.backward()  # Compute gradients
optimizer.step()  # Update weights
```

- **Adam Optimizer**: Adam (short for Adaptive Moment Estimation) is an optimizer that combines the benefits of both **AdaGrad** and **RMSProp**. It is widely used because it adapts the learning rate based on the average of recent gradients.

python

Copy code

```python
optimizer = torch.optim.Adam(model.parameters(), lr=0.001)

# Example: Updating weights using Adam
optimizer.zero_grad()
loss.backward()
optimizer.step()
```

3.3. Backpropagation and Training Neural Networks

Backpropagation is the process of calculating the gradient of the loss function with respect to the model's parameters and updating the parameters using an optimization algorithm.

In PyTorch, **autograd** automatically computes gradients for tensors that have requires_grad=True. After defining a loss function and performing the forward pass, we call the .backward() function to compute gradients. Here's an example:

python

Copy code

```python
# Example of forward pass and backpropagation in a simple model

input_tensor = torch.tensor([[1.0, 2.0]], requires_grad=True)
target = torch.tensor([[1.0]])

# Define a simple model
model = nn.Linear(2, 1)

# Forward pass: compute predicted output
output = model(input_tensor)

# Define loss
loss = nn.MSELoss()(output, target)

# Backward pass: compute gradients
loss.backward()

# Access gradients
```

```python
print(model.weight.grad)
print(model.bias.grad)
```

After calling .backward(), the gradients of the model's parameters are stored in model.weight.grad and model.bias.grad. The optimizer will use these gradients to update the model's parameters.

A typical **training loop** in deep learning consists of the following steps:

1. **Iterating over the dataset**.
2. **Performing forward passes** through the model to compute predictions.
3. **Calculating the loss** between predictions and true values.
4. **Performing backpropagation** to compute gradients.
5. **Updating model parameters** using the optimizer.

Here's how you would structure a typical training loop in PyTorch:

python
Copy code
```python
num_epochs = 10
for epoch in range(num_epochs):
    for data, labels in dataloader:
        optimizer.zero_grad()  # Clear gradients
        predictions = model(data)  # Forward pass
        loss = loss_fn(predictions, labels)  # Compute loss
        loss.backward()  # Backpropagate
        optimizer.step()  # Update weights

    print(f"Epoch [{epoch+1}/{num_epochs}], Loss: {loss.item()}")
```

- **Epoch**: An epoch refers to one complete pass over the entire training dataset. Multiple epochs are required to train a model effectively.
- **Batch**: A batch is a subset of the dataset that is used in one iteration of the training loop. Using smaller batches helps with memory efficiency and speeds up training.
- **Iteration**: An iteration refers to one update of the model's parameters, typically after processing one batch of data.

In this chapter, you have learned how to build neural networks in PyTorch by using **fully connected layers** (nn.Linear), applying **activation functions** (ReLU, Sigmoid, Tanh), and customizing activation functions. You also explored how to use **loss functions** and **optimizers** to train models, along with the essential process of **backpropagation**. Finally, we discussed how to structure a **training loop** and explained the key concepts of **epochs**, **batches**, and **iterations**.

Chapter 4 Regularization Techniques 4.1. Overfitting and Underfitting 4.2. Early Stopping 4.3. Dropout Regularization 4.4. L2 and L1 Regularization (Weight Decay) 4.5. Batch Normalization Write in details and exhaustively on this informatively, using a full length,clear, simple style of writing keeping the language basic and professional. Always ensure all tables, code examples are complete, accurate and well explained

Chapter 4: Regularization Techniques

In deep learning, **regularization** is a technique used to prevent **overfitting** and ensure that the model generalizes well to new, unseen data. In this chapter, we will cover some of the most widely used regularization techniques: **overfitting and underfitting**, **early stopping**, **dropout regularization**, **L2 and L1 regularization (weight decay)**, and **batch normalization**. We will explain these concepts in detail and provide clear, understandable code examples for each.

4.1. Overfitting and Underfitting

Before diving into specific regularization techniques, it is essential to understand the concepts of **overfitting** and **underfitting**.

Overfitting

Overfitting occurs when a model learns the training data too well, including noise and small fluctuations that do not generalize to unseen data. As a result, the model performs very well on the training set but poorly on the validation or test set. Overfitting is a sign that the model is too complex, with too many parameters relative to the number of training examples.

Underfitting

Underfitting occurs when a model is too simple to capture the underlying patterns in the data. This can happen if the model has too few parameters or if the training is not conducted for long enough. The model performs poorly on both the training set and the test set.

Balancing the Two

The goal of regularization is to strike a balance between overfitting and underfitting. The idea is to build a model that is complex enough to capture the data patterns but not so complex that it fits noise. Regularization techniques help by reducing the complexity of the model without sacrificing too much predictive power.

4.2. Early Stopping

Early stopping is a technique that involves monitoring the performance of the model on a validation set during training. If the validation error begins to increase while the training error continues to decrease, the model is likely overfitting. Early stopping halts the training process before the model starts overfitting, saving computational resources and avoiding unnecessary training.

How Early Stopping Works

During training, we track the model's performance on both the **training** and **validation** datasets:

- The model is trained for several epochs.
- If the **validation loss** stops improving for a predefined number of epochs, training is stopped, and the best model (with the lowest validation loss) is kept.

Code Example: Implementing Early Stopping
python
Copy code

```python
import torch
import torch.nn as nn
import torch.optim as optim

# Example model (simple feedforward neural network)
model = nn.Sequential(
    nn.Linear(10, 5),
    nn.ReLU(),
```

```python
    nn.Linear(5, 1)
)

# Optimizer and loss function
optimizer = optim.SGD(model.parameters(), lr=0.01)
loss_fn = nn.MSELoss()

# Early stopping parameters
patience = 5  # Number of epochs to wait before stopping
best_val_loss = float('inf')
epochs_without_improvement = 0

# Simulating training process
for epoch in range(100):
    # Simulated training and validation loss
    train_loss = torch.randn(1)  # Random training loss for
illustration
    val_loss = torch.randn(1)    # Random validation loss for
illustration

    # Check for improvement
    if val_loss < best_val_loss:
        best_val_loss = val_loss
        epochs_without_improvement = 0
    else:
        epochs_without_improvement += 1

    if epochs_without_improvement >= patience:
        print(f"Early stopping at epoch {epoch}")
        break
```

In this example:

- We train the model for a maximum of 100 epochs.
- If the validation loss does not improve for 5 consecutive epochs (patience), we stop training.

4.3. Dropout Regularization

Dropout is a regularization technique that helps prevent overfitting by randomly setting a fraction of the neurons to zero during each forward pass. This prevents the network from becoming overly reliant on any single neuron, forcing the model to learn more robust features.

How Dropout Works

- During training, dropout randomly "drops" units (neurons) in the neural network. Each unit has a probability p of being set to zero.
- During testing, dropout is not applied, but the output of each unit is scaled by the dropout rate to compensate for the units that were dropped during training.

Code Example: Implementing Dropout
python
Copy code

```python
import torch
import torch.nn as nn

# Define a model with Dropout
class DropoutModel(nn.Module):
    def __init__(self):
        super(DropoutModel, self).__init__()
```

```python
        self.fc1 = nn.Linear(10, 5)
        self.dropout = nn.Dropout(0.5)  # 50% probability of
dropping a unit
        self.fc2 = nn.Linear(5, 1)

    def forward(self, x):
        x = torch.relu(self.fc1(x))
        x = self.dropout(x)  # Apply dropout
        x = self.fc2(x)
        return x


# Instantiate and print the model
model = DropoutModel()
print(model)
```

In this model:

- **Dropout(0.5)** means that 50% of the neurons are randomly dropped during training. This regularizes the model and prevents overfitting.

4.4. L2 and L1 Regularization (Weight Decay)

L2 and **L1 regularization** are techniques that add a penalty to the model's loss function based on the size of the model's weights. These penalties help to prevent the model from becoming too complex, thereby reducing overfitting.

L2 Regularization (Weight Decay)

L2 regularization adds a penalty term to the loss function based on the sum of the squared weights. This penalty discourages large weights in the model, making it more likely that the model will generalize well to unseen data. It is often referred to as **weight decay**.

Loss=Loss+λ∑iwi2Loss=Loss+λi∑wi2

Where:

- wiwi are the weights of the model.
- λλ is the regularization hyperparameter that controls the strength of the penalty.

Code Example: Implementing L2 Regularization (Weight Decay)

python

Copy code

```
optimizer = torch.optim.SGD(model.parameters(), lr=0.01,
weight_decay=0.001)  # L2 regularization
```

In this code:

- weight_decay=0.001 applies L2 regularization with a penalty strength of 0.001.

L1 Regularization

L1 regularization adds a penalty based on the sum of the absolute values of the weights:

Loss=Loss+λ∑i|wi|Loss=Loss+λi∑|wi|

L1 regularization tends to promote sparsity, where some of the weights are driven to zero, effectively performing feature selection.

Code Example: Implementing L1 Regularization
python
Copy code

```
l1_lambda = 0.001
l1_norm = sum(p.abs().sum() for p in model.parameters())

loss = loss_fn(output, target) + l1_lambda * l1_norm  # Adding L1
regularization to the loss
```

Here, l1_lambda controls the strength of the L1 regularization, and l1_norm calculates the L1 norm of the model's weights.

4.5. Batch Normalization

Batch normalization is a technique used to normalize the input to each layer in a neural network. This helps to improve training speed, reduce sensitivity to hyperparameters, and potentially lead to better generalization. Batch normalization normalizes the output of a layer by adjusting and scaling it based on the mean and standard deviation of the batch.

How Batch Normalization Works

Batch normalization works by normalizing each mini-batch of data before it is passed through the activation function. The idea is to reduce the internal covariate shift, which occurs when the distribution of inputs to layers changes during training.

The normalized output is then scaled and shifted by learned parameters $\gamma\gamma$ and $\beta\beta$.

$$\hat{x} = x - \mu \sigma \hat{x} = \sigma x - \mu y = \gamma \hat{x} + \beta y = \gamma \hat{x} + \beta$$

Where:

- xx is the input,
- $\mu\mu$ and $\sigma\sigma$ are the mean and standard deviation of the mini-batch,

47

- $\gamma\gamma$ and $\beta\beta$ are learned scaling and shifting parameters.

Code Example: Implementing Batch Normalization
python

Copy code

```python
class BatchNormModel(nn.Module):
  def __init__(self):
    super(BatchNormModel, self).__init__()
    self.fc1 = nn.Linear(10, 5)
    self.bn1 = nn.BatchNorm1d(5)  # Batch Normalization
for 1D input
    self.fc2 = nn.Linear(5, 1)

  def forward(self, x):
    x = torch.relu(self.fc1(x))
    x = self.bn1(x)  # Apply batch normalization
    x = self.fc2(x)
    return x


# Instantiate and print the model
model = BatchNormModel()
print(model)
```

In this example:

- nn.BatchNorm1d(5) applies batch normalization to the output of the first fully connected layer, which has 5 units.

In this chapter, we explored essential regularization techniques to prevent overfitting and improve model generalization. These techniques include **early stopping, dropout regularization, L2 and L1 regularization**, and **batch normalization**. By using these methods, you can control the complexity of your models and ensure that they perform well on unseen data.

Chapter 5: Advanced Training Techniques

In this chapter, we will explore advanced training techniques that are commonly used to improve model performance, training efficiency, and stability. These techniques include **learning rate scheduling**, **gradient clipping**, **mixed precision training**, and **fine-tuning and transfer learning**. These approaches will help you train your models more effectively and ensure that they generalize well to new, unseen data.

5.1. Learning Rate Scheduling

The **learning rate** is a crucial hyperparameter in training deep learning models. It determines the size of the steps the optimizer takes when adjusting the model's weights during training. A high learning rate can cause the model to converge too quickly, potentially overshooting the optimal solution. On the other hand, a learning rate that is too small may cause the model to take too long to converge, possibly getting stuck in a suboptimal solution.

Learning rate scheduling is a technique used to adjust the learning rate during training, typically decreasing it gradually as training progresses. The idea is to start with a relatively high learning rate and reduce it over time to allow the model to fine-tune its weights more precisely as it gets closer to a minimum.

Types of Learning Rate Scheduling

1. **Step Decay**: The learning rate is reduced by a factor after a fixed number of epochs.
2. **Exponential Decay**: The learning rate decreases exponentially over time.
3. **Cosine Annealing**: The learning rate follows a cosine function, decreasing smoothly and periodically.

4. **Reduce on Plateau**: The learning rate is reduced when the validation loss stops improving for a certain number of epochs.

Code Example: Step Decay Learning Rate Scheduling

python

Copy code

```python
import torch
import torch.optim as optim

# Define a simple model and optimizer
model = torch.nn.Linear(10, 1)
optimizer = optim.SGD(model.parameters(), lr=0.1)

# Step learning rate scheduler
scheduler = optim.lr_scheduler.StepLR(optimizer,
step_size=10, gamma=0.1)

# Training loop with learning rate scheduling
for epoch in range(50):
    # Simulated training step
    optimizer.zero_grad()
    # Forward pass, loss calculation, backward pass,
optimizer step (omitted for brevity)
    # optimizer.step()

    # Step the scheduler every epoch
    scheduler.step()
    print(f'Epoch {epoch+1}, Learning Rate:
{scheduler.get_last_lr()}')
```

In this example:

- The learning rate starts at 0.1, and every 10 epochs (step_size=10), the learning rate is reduced by a factor of 0.1 (gamma=0.1).

5.2. Gradient Clipping

Gradient clipping is a technique used to prevent **exploding gradients**, which is a problem that can occur during training, particularly with deep networks or recurrent neural networks (RNNs). Exploding gradients happen when the gradients during backpropagation become excessively large, which can result in unstable updates to the model's weights and prevent the model from converging.

Gradient clipping limits the size of the gradients by scaling them if they exceed a predefined threshold. This keeps the updates from being too large, ensuring that the training process remains stable.

How Gradient Clipping Works

During backpropagation, if the norm of the gradient exceeds a specified threshold, the gradients are rescaled to ensure that their norm is equal to the threshold. This prevents the gradient values from becoming too large.

Code Example: Implementing Gradient Clipping
python
Copy code

```python
import torch
import torch.nn as nn
import torch.optim as optim

# Define a simple model
model = nn.Linear(10, 1)
```

```python
optimizer = optim.SGD(model.parameters(), lr=0.1)

# Simulated training loop
for epoch in range(50):
    optimizer.zero_grad()

    # Simulate some loss and gradients
    input_tensor = torch.randn(10)
    target = torch.randn(1)
    output = model(input_tensor)
    loss = nn.MSELoss()(output, target)

    # Backward pass to compute gradients
    loss.backward()

    # Clip gradients to avoid exploding gradients
    torch.nn.utils.clip_grad_norm_(model.parameters(),
max_norm=1.0)

    # Update the model
    optimizer.step()

    print(f'Epoch {epoch+1}, Loss: {loss.item()}')
```

In this code:

- clip_grad_norm_ is used to clip the gradients of the model's parameters. The max_norm parameter sets the maximum allowed norm of the gradients.

5.3. Mixed Precision Training

Mixed precision training is a technique used to speed up training and reduce memory usage by using lower-precision (16-bit) floating-point numbers for certain computations, rather than the standard 32-bit floating-point numbers (FP32). This can lead to faster training times and less memory usage, especially when working with large models and datasets.

PyTorch supports mixed precision training through the **automatic mixed precision (AMP)** module, which automatically casts operations to lower precision when appropriate and ensures that important operations (like gradient accumulation) are performed in higher precision.

How Mixed Precision Training Works

- **FP16**: The model's weights and most operations are performed using 16-bit precision, which uses less memory and allows faster computation.
- **FP32**: Some operations, such as gradient accumulation, are performed with 32-bit precision to maintain numerical stability.

Code Example: Implementing Mixed Precision Training
python
Copy code

```python
from torch.cuda.amp import autocast, GradScaler

# Initialize the GradScaler for mixed precision
scaler = GradScaler()

# Model and optimizer
model = nn.Linear(10, 1).cuda()
optimizer = optim.Adam(model.parameters(), lr=0.001)
```

```python
# Training loop with mixed precision
for epoch in range(50):
    optimizer.zero_grad()

    # Forward pass with autocast for mixed precision
    with autocast():
        input_tensor = torch.randn(10).cuda()
        target = torch.randn(1).cuda()
        output = model(input_tensor)
        loss = nn.MSELoss()(output, target)

    # Scale the loss and perform backward pass
    scaler.scale(loss).backward()

    # Update the model parameters
    scaler.step(optimizer)
    scaler.update()  # Update the scale for the next step

    print(f'Epoch {epoch+1}, Loss: {loss.item()}')
```

In this example:

- **autocast()** is used to perform the forward pass in mixed precision.
- **GradScaler()** is used to scale the loss and gradients to prevent underflow during the backward pass.

5.4. Fine-Tuning and Transfer Learning

Fine-tuning and **transfer learning** are techniques used to leverage pre-trained models for a variety of tasks, especially when training from scratch is computationally expensive or when limited labeled data is available.

Transfer learning involves taking a model that has been pre-trained on a large dataset (such as ImageNet) and adapting it to a new task. Pre-trained models have already learned useful features from the original task, which can be transferred to a new task.

The idea is to use the pre-trained model as a feature extractor and fine-tune it for the new task.

Code Example: Using a Pre-trained Model for Transfer Learning
python
Copy code

```python
import torchvision.models as models
import torch.nn as nn

# Load a pre-trained ResNet18 model
model = models.resnet18(pretrained=True)

# Freeze the early layers to retain learned features
for param in model.parameters():
    param.requires_grad = False

# Replace the last layer with a new one for the new task
model.fc = nn.Linear(model.fc.in_features, 2)  # Assuming a binary classification task

# Print the modified model
```

```
print(model)
```

In this example:

- We load a pre-trained **ResNet18** model.
- We freeze the layers by setting requires_grad=False, so the weights of these layers are not updated during training.
- We replace the final fully connected layer to match the number of output classes for the new task.

Fine-tuning involves unfreezing some layers of the pre-trained model and training them on the new task. The commonly used strategy is to freeze the earlier layers (which capture general features) and fine-tune the deeper layers (which capture more task-specific features).

Code Example: Fine-Tuning Pre-trained Model
python
Copy code

```python
# Freeze all layers initially
for param in model.parameters():
    param.requires_grad = False


# Unfreeze the last few layers for fine-tuning
for param in model.layer4.parameters():
    param.requires_grad = True


# Now, only the last few layers will be updated during training
optimizer = torch.optim.SGD(model.parameters(), lr=0.001)
```

Example training loop (omitted for brevity)

In this example:

- We freeze all layers except for the last block (layer4) of the pre-trained model.
- By doing so, we reduce the number of trainable parameters, which can help avoid overfitting and improve training efficiency.

In this chapter, we covered **advanced training techniques** that can significantly improve model performance and training efficiency. We explored **learning rate scheduling** to adjust the learning rate during training, **gradient clipping** to handle exploding gradients, **mixed precision training** to speed up training and reduce memory usage, and **fine-tuning and transfer learning** to leverage pre-trained models for new tasks. These techniques will help you train deep learning models more effectively, especially when dealing with large datasets and complex architectures.

Part 3

Intermediate Deep Learning Models

Chapter 6: Convolutional Neural Networks (CNNs)

Convolutional Neural Networks (CNNs) are one of the most widely used architectures in deep learning, particularly for tasks such as image classification, object detection, and more. CNNs excel at automatically learning spatial hierarchies of features in images through their use of convolutional layers. This chapter will introduce you to the essential components of CNNs, show you how to implement them in PyTorch, and explore some advanced CNN architectures such as VGG, ResNet, and Inception networks.

6.1. Introduction to CNNs

CNNs are designed to process data that comes in the form of grids, such as images, which are essentially 2D grids of pixels. Unlike fully connected networks that treat input as a flat vector, CNNs take advantage of the spatial structure in images, learning local patterns such as edges, textures, and more complex patterns in higher layers.

The core component of a CNN is the **convolutional layer**. In a convolutional layer, a small matrix (called a **filter** or **kernel**) slides over the input image, performing element-wise multiplications and summing the results to produce a single output value. This operation is repeated for each region of the image, creating a **feature map** that represents the presence of certain features in the image.

The primary advantages of using convolutional layers are:

1. **Local Receptive Field**: Each neuron only looks at a small local region of the image, which reduces the number of parameters and captures local patterns.
2. **Weight Sharing**: The same filter is applied to different regions of the image, which reduces the number of parameters and makes the model more efficient.

Example of Convolution Operation:

Consider a 3x3 filter and a 5x5 input image:

markdown
Copy code
Input Image (5x5):

1 2 3 4 5
6 7 8 9 10
11 12 13 14 15
16 17 18 19 20
21 22 23 24 25

Filter (3x3):
1 0 -1
1 0 -1
1 0 -1

Output Feature Map (3x3):
(1*1 + 2*0 + 3*(-1) + 6*1 + 7*0 + 8*(-1) + 11*1 + 12*0 + 13*(-1))
= -12

...

This operation is repeated across the entire image, producing a feature map that highlights the detected features.

In PyTorch, you can use the nn.Conv2d class to define a 2D convolutional layer:

python
Copy code
```python
import torch
```

```
import torch.nn as nn

# Example: 1 input channel (grayscale), 3 output channels
(feature maps), 3x3 filter
conv_layer = nn.Conv2d(1, 3, kernel_size=3)

# Sample input (1 image, 1 channel, 5x5)
input_image = torch.randn(1, 1, 5, 5)

# Apply the convolutional layer
output = conv_layer(input_image)
print(output.shape)  # Output shape: [1, 3, 3, 3]
```

In this code:

- 1 input channel (grayscale image).
- 3 output channels (3 different feature maps).
- A 3x3 kernel.

Pooling is a downsampling operation used to reduce the spatial dimensions (height and width) of the feature maps while retaining important information. Pooling helps to reduce computational complexity and the risk of overfitting.

- **Max Pooling**: For each region of the image, max pooling selects the maximum value. This operation captures the most prominent features in the image.
- **Average Pooling**: Instead of taking the maximum value, average pooling computes the average of values in the region.

Max Pooling Example:

For a 2x2 region, max pooling will take the maximum value:

mathematica

Copy code

Input Feature Map (4x4):

```
1  2  3  4
5  6  7  8
9  10 11 12
13 14 15 16
```

Max Pooling (2x2):

Max(1, 2, 5, 6) = 6, Max(3, 4, 7, 8) = 8

Max(9, 10, 13, 14) = 14, Max(11, 12, 15, 16) = 16

Output Feature Map (2x2):

```
6  8
14 16
```

In PyTorch, max pooling can be implemented using nn.MaxPool2d:

python

Copy code

```python
max_pool = nn.MaxPool2d(kernel_size=2)

# Sample input (1 image, 1 channel, 4x4 feature map)
input_feature_map = torch.randn(1, 1, 4, 4)

# Apply max pooling
output = max_pool(input_feature_map)
print(output.shape)  # Output shape: [1, 1, 2, 2]
```

Here, kernel_size=2 means pooling is performed on 2x2 regions.

After passing through several convolutional and pooling layers, the resulting feature maps are flattened into a vector and passed through one or more **fully connected (FC) layers**. The FC layers are responsible for combining the learned features and making predictions based on them.

The last fully connected layer typically maps the flattened features to the desired output size (e.g., the number of classes in a classification task).

6.2. Implementing CNNs in PyTorch

Now that we have covered the basic components of CNNs, let's move on to implementing them in PyTorch.

A basic CNN consists of a series of convolutional layers, pooling layers, and fully connected layers. Let's define a simple CNN for image classification.

python
Copy code
```python
import torch
import torch.nn as nn


class SimpleCNN(nn.Module):
    def __init__(self):
        super(SimpleCNN, self).__init__()

        # Convolutional Layer 1
        self.conv1 = nn.Conv2d(1, 32, kernel_size=3, padding=1)
        self.pool = nn.MaxPool2d(kernel_size=2, stride=2)
```

```python
    # Convolutional Layer 2
    self.conv2 = nn.Conv2d(32, 64, kernel_size=3,
padding=1)


    # Fully Connected Layers
    self.fc1 = nn.Linear(64 * 7 * 7, 128)  # Assuming input
image size is 28x28
    self.fc2 = nn.Linear(128, 10)  # Output 10 classes for
classification

  def forward(self, x):
    # Apply convolutional and pooling layers
    x = self.pool(torch.relu(self.conv1(x)))
    x = self.pool(torch.relu(self.conv2(x)))

    # Flatten the tensor for the fully connected layer
    x = x.view(-1, 64 * 7 * 7)

    # Apply fully connected layers
    x = torch.relu(self.fc1(x))
    x = self.fc2(x)
    return x

# Instantiate the model
model = SimpleCNN()
print(model)
```

In this example:

- The model consists of two convolutional layers (conv1, conv2) followed by two fully connected layers (fc1, fc2).
- The input image is assumed to be a 28x28 grayscale image (e.g., MNIST).
- The output of the last fully connected layer has 10 units (for a 10-class classification task).

Once the CNN model is defined, we can train it on an image dataset like MNIST. Here's a simplified training loop to train the model:

python

Copy code

```python
import torch.optim as optim
from torch.utils.data import DataLoader
from torchvision import datasets, transforms

# Define data transforms for training and testing
transform = transforms.Compose([transforms.ToTensor(),
transforms.Normalize((0.5,), (0.5,))])

# Download and load the MNIST dataset
train_dataset = datasets.MNIST(root='./data', train=True,
download=True, transform=transform)
train_loader = DataLoader(train_dataset, batch_size=64,
shuffle=True)

# Instantiate the model, loss function, and optimizer
model = SimpleCNN()
loss_fn = nn.CrossEntropyLoss()
optimizer = optim.Adam(model.parameters(), lr=0.001)

# Training loop
for epoch in range(10):  # 10 epochs
```

```python
model.train()  # Set the model to training mode
running_loss = 0.0

for inputs, labels in train_loader:
    optimizer.zero_grad()  # Clear previous gradients

    # Forward pass
    outputs = model(inputs)

    # Compute the loss
    loss = loss_fn(outputs, labels)

    # Backward pass
    loss.backward()

    # Update the weights
    optimizer.step()

    running_loss += loss.item()

    print(f'Epoch {epoch+1}, Loss: {running_loss / len(train_loader)}')
```

In this code:

- We use the **MNIST** dataset and apply basic transformations (converting images to tensors and normalizing).
- The model is trained for 10 epochs using **Adam optimizer** and **cross-entropy loss**.

6.3. Advanced CNN Architectures

While simple CNNs can achieve good performance on small datasets, more complex architectures have been developed for handling larger and more challenging tasks. Let's take a look at three widely used advanced CNN architectures: **VGG**, **ResNet**, and **Inception**.

VGG Networks are known for their simplicity and depth. The key characteristic of VGG is the use of **3x3 convolutional filters** stacked on top of each other, which increases the depth of the network while maintaining a simple structure. VGG-16 and VGG-19 are two popular variants of this architecture, with 16 and 19 layers, respectively.

- VGG uses small filters (3x3) and increases depth by stacking more convolutional layers.

ResNet (Residual Networks) introduced the concept of **skip connections**, which allow the model to bypass one or more layers and directly pass information from earlier layers to later ones. This helps in training very deep networks by mitigating the vanishing gradient problem.

- The core idea of ResNet is the **residual block**, which adds the input to the output of a few layers.

python
Copy code

```python
import torchvision.models as models
resnet_model = models.resnet18(pretrained=True)
print(resnet_model)
```

- In ResNet, layers are grouped into residual blocks, and the outputs are added to the input before passing through subsequent layers.

Inception Networks (also known as GoogLeNet) introduced the **Inception module**, which allows the network to use multiple filter sizes (1x1, 3x3, 5x5) in parallel at each layer. This allows the network to capture different levels of feature representations at the same layer.

- The Inception architecture uses a mixture of convolutions with different kernel sizes in the same layer.

python

Copy code

```
inception_model = models.inception_v3(pretrained=True)
print(inception_model)
```

In this chapter, we introduced the core components of **Convolutional Neural Networks (CNNs)**, including **convolutional layers**, **pooling layers**, and **fully connected layers**. We also walked through the implementation of a simple CNN in PyTorch and demonstrated how to train it for image classification tasks. Finally, we explored advanced CNN architectures such as **VGG**, **ResNet**, and **Inception networks**, which are used for more complex tasks and larger datasets.

Chapter 7: Recurrent Neural Networks (RNNs) and LSTMs

Recurrent Neural Networks (RNNs) and Long Short-Term Memory (LSTM) networks are widely used for tasks involving sequential data, such as time-series forecasting, natural language processing (NLP), and speech recognition. RNNs and LSTMs are capable of maintaining a memory of past inputs, which makes them suitable for modeling time-dependent information. In this chapter, we will discuss RNNs and LSTMs in detail, cover their implementation in PyTorch, and explore their applications in various domains.

7.1. Introduction to RNNs

A **Recurrent Neural Network (RNN)** is a type of neural network designed for processing sequential data. Unlike traditional feedforward neural networks, RNNs have connections that loop back on themselves, which allows them to maintain a hidden state that captures information from previous time steps. This hidden state is updated at each time step based on the current input and the previous state, making RNNs capable of modeling sequential dependencies.

How RNNs Work

At each time step t, the RNN takes an input x_t and updates its hidden state h_t as follows:

$$h_t = f(W_h \cdot h_{t-1} + W_x \cdot x_t + b)$$

Where:

- h_{t-1} is the hidden state from the previous time step,
- x_t is the input at time step t,

- $W_h$$W_h$ and $W_x$$W_x$ are the weights for the hidden state and the input,
- $b$$b$ is the bias term, and
- $f$$f$ is an activation function (typically **tanh** or **ReLU**).

The RNN produces an output $y_t$$y_t$ based on the hidden state at each time step. However, basic RNNs suffer from issues like **vanishing gradients**, which makes training on long sequences difficult.

7.2. Long Short-Term Memory (LSTM) Networks

Long Short-Term Memory (LSTM) networks were introduced to address the issues of vanishing gradients in basic RNNs. LSTMs are a specialized type of RNN designed to capture long-range dependencies in sequential data. They achieve this by using **gates** that control the flow of information and regulate the memory of the network. These gates allow LSTMs to remember relevant information for long periods and forget irrelevant information.

Components of an LSTM Cell

An LSTM cell consists of the following components:

- **Forget Gate**: Decides which information from the previous hidden state should be discarded.
- **Input Gate**: Determines what new information should be added to the memory cell.
- **Cell State**: Carries long-term memory through the network, allowing information to be passed from one time step to the next.
- **Output Gate**: Decides what part of the memory cell should be output as the hidden state for the current time step.

The equations governing the LSTM cell are as follows:

1. **Forget Gate**:
   $f_t=\sigma(W_f\cdot[h_{t-1},x_t]+b_f)f_t=\sigma(W_f[h_{t-1},x_t]+b_f)$

2. **Input Gate**:
   $i_t=\sigma(W_i\cdot[h_{t-1},x_t]+b_i)i_t=\sigma(W_i\cdot[h_{t-1},x_t]+b_i$
   $)C_t\sim=\tanh(W_C\cdot[h_{t-1},x_t]+b_C)C_t\sim=\tanh(W_C\cdot[h_{t-1},x_t]+b_C)$

3. **Cell State Update**:
   $C_t=f_t\cdot C_{t-1}+i_t\cdot C_t\sim C_t=f_t\cdot C_{t-1}+i_t\cdot C_t\sim$

4. **Output Gate**:
   $o_t=\sigma(W_o\cdot[h_{t-1},x_t]+b_o)o_t=\sigma(W_o\cdot[h_{t-1},x_t]+b_o)h_t=o_t\cdot\tanh(C_t)h_t$
   $=o_t\cdot\tanh(C_t)$

Where:

- $\sigma\sigma$ is the **sigmoid** activation function, which outputs values between 0 and 1,
- $\tanh\tanh$ is the **hyperbolic tangent** function, used to control the scale of the memory cell.

By learning which information to keep and which to forget at each time step, LSTMs can capture long-range dependencies more effectively than basic RNNs.

7.3. Implementing RNNs and LSTMs in PyTorch

In PyTorch, RNNs and LSTMs are implemented using the nn.RNN and nn.LSTM classes, respectively. These classes provide an easy way to create RNN and LSTM layers and include various options for customizing the architecture.

Let's implement a simple RNN for sequence classification using PyTorch.

python
Copy code

```python
import torch
import torch.nn as nn

# Define a simple RNN model
class SimpleRNN(nn.Module):
    def __init__(self, input_size, hidden_size, output_size):
        super(SimpleRNN, self).__init__()
        self.rnn = nn.RNN(input_size, hidden_size, batch_first=True)
        self.fc = nn.Linear(hidden_size, output_size)

    def forward(self, x):
        # Pass input through RNN
        rnn_out, _ = self.rnn(x)  # Ignore hidden state (for simplicity)
        # Use the last time step's output for classification
        out = self.fc(rnn_out[:, -1, :])
        return out

# Example usage
input_size = 10  # Number of input features
hidden_size = 50  # Number of hidden units
output_size = 1  # Output size (e.g., for binary classification)

# Instantiate the model
model = SimpleRNN(input_size, hidden_size, output_size)

# Sample input (batch_size=5, sequence_length=20, input_size=10)
input_tensor = torch.randn(5, 20, 10)
```

```python
# Forward pass
output = model(input_tensor)
print(output)
```

In this example:

- The RNN layer processes input sequences and produces hidden states.
- The output from the last time step is passed through a fully connected layer for classification.

Next, let's implement a simple LSTM for sequence classification.

python

Copy code

```python
class SimpleLSTM(nn.Module):
    def __init__(self, input_size, hidden_size, output_size):
        super(SimpleLSTM, self).__init__()
        self.lstm = nn.LSTM(input_size, hidden_size, batch_first=True)
        self.fc = nn.Linear(hidden_size, output_size)

    def forward(self, x):
        # Pass input through LSTM
        lstm_out, _ = self.lstm(x)  # Ignore hidden state (for simplicity)
        # Use the last time step's output for classification
        out = self.fc(lstm_out[:, -1, :])
        return out

# Example usage
```

```
model = SimpleLSTM(input_size, hidden_size, output_size)

# Sample input (batch_size=5, sequence_length=20,
input_size=10)
input_tensor = torch.randn(5, 20, 10)

# Forward pass
output = model(input_tensor)
print(output)
```

In this LSTM example:

- We use the LSTM layer to process sequences and produce hidden states.
- The output of the last time step is passed to a fully connected layer to make predictions.

7.4. Applications of RNNs and LSTMs

RNNs and LSTMs are particularly useful for tasks involving sequential data, where the order of inputs matters. Here are two key areas where RNNs and LSTMs are widely used:

Time-Series Prediction

Time-series data consists of sequences of data points indexed in time order. Applications include forecasting stock prices, weather prediction, and energy consumption prediction.

For time-series prediction, RNNs and LSTMs are used to model the dependencies between past and future data points.

Natural Language Processing (NLP)

In NLP, RNNs and LSTMs are used for tasks such as:

- **Sentiment Analysis**: Analyzing text to determine whether the sentiment is positive, negative, or neutral.
- **Machine Translation**: Translating text from one language to another by processing sequences of words.
- **Text Generation**: Generating new text sequences based on the patterns learned from a corpus of text.

LSTMs are especially useful in NLP because they can capture long-range dependencies in text, such as relationships between words that are far apart.

7.5. Bi-directional RNNs and GRUs

Bi-directional RNNs

A **bi-directional RNN** processes the sequence in both forward and backward directions, which allows the network to capture information from both the past and the future. This is especially useful in tasks like machine translation, where both the previous and next words in a sequence provide valuable context.

In PyTorch, bi-directional RNNs can be implemented by setting the bidirectional=True parameter.

python

Copy code

```python
class BiRNN(nn.Module):
    def __init__(self, input_size, hidden_size, output_size):
        super(BiRNN, self).__init__()
        self.rnn = nn.RNN(input_size, hidden_size, batch_first=True, bidirectional=True)
```

```python
        self.fc = nn.Linear(hidden_size * 2, output_size)  #
Multiply by 2 for bi-directional

    def forward(self, x):
        rnn_out, _ = self.rnn(x)
        out = self.fc(rnn_out[:, -1, :])
        return out
```

GRUs (Gated Recurrent Units)

GRUs are a simplified version of LSTMs. While LSTMs use three
gates (forget, input, output), GRUs combine the forget and input gates
into a single update gate, making them computationally more
efficient. GRUs perform similarly to LSTMs but are often faster to
train and require fewer parameters.

In PyTorch, GRUs can be implemented using nn.GRU:

python
Copy code
```python
class SimpleGRU(nn.Module):
    def __init__(self, input_size, hidden_size, output_size):
        super(SimpleGRU, self).__init__()
        self.gru = nn.GRU(input_size, hidden_size,
batch_first=True)
        self.fc = nn.Linear(hidden_size, output_size)

    def forward(self, x):
        gru_out, _ = self.gru(x)
        out = self.fc(gru_out[:, -1, :])
        return out
```

In this chapter, we covered **Recurrent Neural Networks (RNNs)** and **Long Short-Term Memory (LSTM)** networks, which are particularly effective for tasks involving sequential data. We discussed how RNNs and LSTMs work, their components, and how to implement them in PyTorch. We also explored their applications in **time-series prediction** and **natural language processing (NLP)**. Finally, we introduced **bi-directional RNNs** and **GRUs**, which offer more flexibility and efficiency in modeling sequential dependencies.

Chapter 8: Transformers and Attention Mechanisms

Transformers have revolutionized the field of natural language processing (NLP) and sequence-based tasks. Their ability to capture long-range dependencies and process sequences in parallel has made them the architecture of choice for tasks such as machine translation, text generation, and question answering. In this chapter, we will dive deep into **attention mechanisms**, which are at the heart of the Transformer architecture. We will also explore the implementation of Transformers in PyTorch, their architecture, and popular Transformer models like **BERT** and **GPT**.

8.1. Understanding Attention Mechanisms

The key innovation behind the Transformer model is the **attention mechanism**. Attention mechanisms allow the model to focus on different parts of the input sequence with varying attention at each time step, rather than processing the sequence in a fixed, sequential manner. This capability enables the model to capture dependencies between distant tokens in the input sequence effectively.

At its core, an attention layer computes a weighted sum of input values (usually embeddings or feature maps) where the weights are determined by a similarity function between a **query** and a set of **keys**. The output of the attention mechanism is the weighted sum of values, where the weights (attention scores) determine the importance of each value.

The attention mechanism is typically defined by the following steps:

1. **Compute the Query, Key, and Value**: For each input, the model generates three vectors:
   - The **query** vector Q,

- The **key** vector KK,
- The **value** vector VV.

2. **Calculate the Attention Scores**: The attention score is computed as the dot product between the query and key vectors. The scores are then scaled, typically by the square root of the dimension of the key vectors, to prevent large values that could lead to instability during training.
3. **Softmax**: The scores are passed through the **softmax** function to normalize them, turning them into a probability distribution.
4. **Weighted Sum**: The output is obtained by computing the weighted sum of the value vectors using the attention scores as weights.

Mathematically, the attention output is computed as:

$\text{Attention}(Q,K,V) = \text{Softmax}(\frac{QK^T}{\sqrt{d_k}})V$

Where:

- QQ, KK, and VV are the query, key, and value matrices, respectively,
- d_k is the dimension of the key vector.

- **Self-Attention**: In **self-attention**, the query, key, and value vectors come from the same input sequence. The attention mechanism allows each token in the sequence to focus on other tokens, capturing dependencies across the sequence. This is crucial for tasks like machine translation, where the meaning of a word may depend on other words in the sentence.
- **Multi-Head Attention**: Multi-head attention extends the self-attention mechanism by using multiple attention heads. Each head performs its own attention operation with different sets of learnable parameters, allowing the model to capture different types of relationships between tokens. The outputs of

all heads are concatenated and passed through a linear layer to produce the final attention output.

The advantage of multi-head attention is that it allows the model to attend to different parts of the sequence in parallel, capturing various aspects of the relationships between tokens.

Code Example: Self-Attention in PyTorch
python

Copy code

```python
import torch
import torch.nn as nn


class SelfAttention(nn.Module):
    def __init__(self, embed_size, heads):
        super(SelfAttention, self).__init__()
        self.embed_size = embed_size
        self.heads = heads
        self.head_dim = embed_size // heads

        assert self.head_dim * heads == embed_size, "Embedding size must be divisible by number of heads"

        self.values = nn.Linear(self.head_dim, embed_size, bias=False)
        self.keys = nn.Linear(self.head_dim, embed_size, bias=False)
        self.queries = nn.Linear(self.head_dim, embed_size, bias=False)
        self.fc_out = nn.Linear(heads * self.head_dim, embed_size)
```

```python
    def forward(self, values, keys, query, mask):
        N = query.shape[0]  # Batch size
        value_len, key_len, query_len = values.shape[1],
keys.shape[1], query.shape[1]

        # Split the embedding into self.heads different pieces
        values = values.reshape(N, value_len, self.heads,
self.head_dim)
        keys = keys.reshape(N, key_len, self.heads,
self.head_dim)
        query = query.reshape(N, query_len, self.heads,
self.head_dim)

        # Scaled dot-product attention
        energy = torch.einsum("nqhd,nkhd->nhqk", [query,
keys])  # (N, heads, query_len, key_len)
        if mask is not None:
            energy = energy.masked_fill(mask == 0, float("-
1e20"))

        attention = torch.softmax(energy / (self.head_dim ** (1
/ 2)), dim=3)  # Normalize energy
        out = torch.einsum("nhql,nlhd->nqhd", [attention,
values])  # (N, query_len, heads, head_dim)

        out = out.reshape(N, query_len, self.heads *
self.head_dim)
        out = self.fc_out(out)  # Linear layer to combine heads
        return out

# Example of usage
```

```python
embed_size = 256
heads = 8
attention = SelfAttention(embed_size, heads)

# Example inputs (batch_size=2, seq_len=10,
embed_size=256)
values = torch.rand(2, 10, embed_size)
keys = torch.rand(2, 10, embed_size)
query = torch.rand(2, 10, embed_size)

output = attention(values, keys, query, mask=None)
print(output.shape)  # Output shape: (2, 10, 256)
```

In this code:

- We define a **SelfAttention** class, which implements the self-attention mechanism.
- The attention scores are computed using the scaled dot-product method, followed by a softmax normalization.
- The outputs of the attention heads are concatenated and passed through a linear layer to produce the final result.

8.2. Implementing Transformers in PyTorch

Now that we have a solid understanding of attention mechanisms, let's look at how to implement the full **Transformer architecture** in PyTorch.

The Transformer architecture consists of two main components: the **encoder** and the **decoder**. The encoder processes the input sequence, and the decoder generates the output sequence. Each encoder and decoder layer includes multi-head self-attention, feedforward layers, and normalization layers.

A typical Transformer consists of:

1. **Multi-Head Self-Attention**: Each token attends to all other tokens in the input sequence.
2. **Positional Encoding**: Since Transformers do not inherently process sequential data like RNNs, positional encoding is added to the input embeddings to provide information about the position of tokens in the sequence.
3. **Feedforward Layers**: These are fully connected layers applied independently to each token.

The Transformer architecture is designed using an **encoder-decoder** structure. The encoder processes the input sequence and generates a set of encoded representations. The decoder takes these representations and generates the output sequence.

Here is an example of how to implement a Transformer encoder-decoder model in PyTorch:

python
Copy code

```python
import torch
import torch.nn as nn


class Transformer(nn.Module):
    def __init__(self, embed_size, heads, num_layers,
input_vocab_size, output_vocab_size, dropout=0.1):
        super(Transformer, self).__init__()
        self.encoder = nn.TransformerEncoder(
            nn.TransformerEncoderLayer(d_model=embed_size,
nhead=heads, dropout=dropout),
            num_layers
```

```python
        )
        self.decoder = nn.TransformerDecoder(
            nn.TransformerDecoderLayer(d_model=embed_size,
nhead=heads, dropout=dropout),
            num_layers
        )
        self.src_tok_emb = nn.Embedding(input_vocab_size,
embed_size)
        self.tgt_tok_emb = nn.Embedding(output_vocab_size,
embed_size)
        self.positional_encoding = nn.Parameter(torch.rand(1,
embed_size))
        self.fc_out = nn.Linear(embed_size,
output_vocab_size)

    def forward(self, src, tgt, src_mask=None,
tgt_mask=None):
        src_emb = self.src_tok_emb(src) +
self.positional_encoding
        tgt_emb = self.tgt_tok_emb(tgt) +
self.positional_encoding
        memory = self.encoder(src_emb,
src_key_padding_mask=src_mask)
        output = self.decoder(tgt_emb, memory,
tgt_mask=tgt_mask,
memory_key_padding_mask=src_mask)
        return self.fc_out(output)

# Example usage
model = Transformer(embed_size=512, heads=8,
num_layers=6, input_vocab_size=10000,
output_vocab_size=10000)
```

```python
# Example input (batch_size=32, seq_len=10)
src = torch.randint(0, 10000, (32, 10))  # Random input
sequence
tgt = torch.randint(0, 10000, (32, 10))  # Random output
sequence

output = model(src, tgt)
print(output.shape)  # Output shape: (32, 10, 10000)
```

In this code:

- We define a Transformer model with an encoder and decoder using nn.TransformerEncoder and nn.TransformerDecoder.
- We use **positional encoding** to add information about the position of tokens in the sequence.

8.3. Transformers for NLP (BERT, GPT)

Two of the most well-known Transformer-based models in NLP are **BERT (Bidirectional Encoder Representations from Transformers)** and **GPT (Generative Pretrained Transformer)**. These models leverage the Transformer architecture to perform a variety of NLP tasks.

BERT:

- BERT is a **pre-trained** model that learns bidirectional context by training on large corpora. It uses the Transformer encoder to understand the context of each word in a sentence by considering both the words before and after it.

- BERT is typically fine-tuned for downstream tasks like **question answering, text classification**, and **named entity recognition (NER)**.

GPT:

- GPT, on the other hand, is a **causal (unidirectional) language model**, which predicts the next word in a sequence based on the words before it. GPT uses the Transformer decoder and has been highly successful in text generation tasks.

8.4. Fine-Tuning Transformer Models in PyTorch

Fine-tuning pre-trained Transformer models like BERT and GPT on specific tasks is a common practice in NLP. PyTorch provides several pre-trained models through the transformers library (by Hugging Face), which makes it easy to fine-tune these models.

Code Example: Fine-Tuning BERT for Text Classification python

Copy code

```python
from transformers import BertForSequenceClassification, AdamW
from torch.utils.data import DataLoader
from transformers import BertTokenizer


# Load pre-trained BERT model and tokenizer
model = BertForSequenceClassification.from_pretrained('bert-base-uncased')
tokenizer = BertTokenizer.from_pretrained('bert-base-uncased')
```

```python
# Sample input text
text = ["Hello, how are you?", "I am fine, thank you!"]
labels = [1, 0]  # Example binary labels

# Tokenize the input text
inputs = tokenizer(text, padding=True, truncation=True,
return_tensors="pt")

# Example DataLoader (batching input text)
dataset =
torch.utils.data.TensorDataset(inputs['input_ids'],
inputs['attention_mask'], torch.tensor(labels))
dataloader = DataLoader(dataset, batch_size=2)

# Fine-tuning the model
optimizer = AdamW(model.parameters(), lr=2e-5)

for epoch in range(3):
    for batch in dataloader:
        optimizer.zero_grad()

        input_ids, attention_mask, label = batch

        # Forward pass
        outputs = model(input_ids,
attention_mask=attention_mask, labels=label)

        # Compute loss and backpropagate
        loss = outputs.loss
        loss.backward()
```

```
optimizer.step()

print(f"Epoch {epoch+1}, Loss: {loss.item()}")
```

In this example:

- We load the pre-trained **BERT model** for sequence classification using the transformers library.
- We tokenize the input text and fine-tune the model using a **DataLoader** to batch the inputs.

In this chapter, we covered the **attention mechanism**, the heart of the **Transformer architecture**. We explored how self-attention and multi-head attention work, as well as how to implement Transformers in PyTorch. We also discussed the practical use of Transformers for NLP tasks using models like **BERT** and **GPT**, and how to fine-tune these models for specific tasks.

Chapter 9: Generative Models

Generative models are a class of machine learning models designed to generate new data that is similar to a given dataset. They are used in a variety of applications such as image generation, style transfer, data augmentation, and more. In this chapter, we will explore two of the most popular types of generative models: **Variational Autoencoders (VAEs)** and **Generative Adversarial Networks (GANs)**. We will discuss their theory, implementation in PyTorch, and explore their applications in various domains.

9.1. Variational Autoencoders (VAEs)

A **Variational Autoencoder (VAE)** is a generative model that combines deep learning with probabilistic graphical models. It is an extension of the traditional **autoencoder**, which is designed to learn an efficient representation (encoding) of input data. However, VAEs learn a probabilistic distribution over the data instead of a fixed encoding, which allows them to generate new samples from that distribution.

VAEs consist of two main components:

1. **Encoder**: The encoder takes an input (such as an image) and encodes it into a lower-dimensional latent space. However, rather than mapping the input to a fixed point, the encoder outputs a **mean** and **variance** for a distribution in the latent space, typically a **Gaussian distribution**.
2. **Decoder**: The decoder takes samples from the latent distribution and reconstructs the original data. This means that instead of directly reconstructing an image, the decoder generates new data based on the latent representation.

The objective of a VAE is to maximize the **variational lower bound** (also known as the ELBO), which is the sum of two parts:

- **Reconstruction loss**: Measures how well the decoder reconstructs the input data.
- **KL Divergence**: Measures how close the learned latent distribution is to the prior distribution (usually a standard normal distribution).

The total loss function is:

Loss=Reconstruction Loss+KL DivergenceLoss=Reconstruction Loss+KL Divergence

In PyTorch, we can build a simple VAE using nn.Module. Let's implement a basic VAE for image generation (e.g., using the MNIST dataset).

Code Example: VAE Implementation
python
Copy code

```python
import torch
import torch.nn as nn
import torch.optim as optim
from torch.utils.data import DataLoader
from torchvision import datasets, transforms

class VAE(nn.Module):
    def __init__(self, latent_dim=2):
        super(VAE, self).__init__()
        self.fc1 = nn.Linear(28 * 28, 400)  # Encoder
        self.fc21 = nn.Linear(400, latent_dim)  # Mean of latent space
        self.fc22 = nn.Linear(400, latent_dim)  # Log-variance of latent space
        self.fc3 = nn.Linear(latent_dim, 400)  # Decoder
```

```python
        self.fc4 = nn.Linear(400, 28 * 28)  # Final
reconstruction

    def encode(self, x):
        h1 = torch.relu(self.fc1(x))
        return self.fc21(h1), self.fc22(h1)

    def reparameterize(self, mu, logvar):
        std = torch.exp(0.5*logvar)
        eps = torch.randn_like(std)
        return mu + eps*std

    def decode(self, z):
        h3 = torch.relu(self.fc3(z))
        return torch.sigmoid(self.fc4(h3))  # Sigmoid for output
in [0, 1]

    def forward(self, x):
        mu, logvar = self.encode(x.view(-1, 28*28))
        z = self.reparameterize(mu, logvar)
        return self.decode(z), mu, logvar

 def loss_function(recon_x, x, mu, logvar):
    BCE = nn.BCELoss(reduction='sum')(recon_x, x.view(-1,
28*28))
    # KL divergence
    # See: Kingma & Welling, 2013
    # https://arxiv.org/abs/1312.6114
    # KL(q(z|x)||p(z)) = 0.5 * sum(1 + log(sigma^2) - mu^2 -
sigma^2)
```

```python
# where sigma = exp(0.5*logvar)
# In PyTorch, the implementation is numerically stable
# when we compute the KL divergence in the latent space
# using log variance rather than variance.
# The term becomes the difference between the Gaussian
# approximations to the prior and posterior distribution.
# We want to minimize this KL divergence, hence the
negation.
# Thus the full loss function is a weighted sum:
# Recon_loss + KL_loss
# with a positive weight for the KL divergence
# (since we aim to prevent a posterior too far from a
standard normal)
# Tuning this term is important.
# More details on this at
https://pytorch.org/docs/stable/nn.functional.html#torch.
nn.functional.kl_div
#
# Use this implementation if you're using this code for a
VAE


# The loss for KL divergence:
# KL(q(z|x)||p(z)) = 0.5 * sum(1 + log(sigma^2) - mu^2 -
sigma^2)
# where sigma = exp(0.5*logvar)
# The values are constant, hence need adjustment for
each term
# in respect for this mechanism.


# We conclude with the sum
# return full loss function
```

```python
    return BCE + 0.5 * torch.sum(torch.exp(logvar) + mu**2 - 1 - logvar)


# Instantiate model, optimizer, and dataset
model = VAE(latent_dim=2)
optimizer = optim.Adam(model.parameters(), lr=1e-3)
train_loader = DataLoader(datasets.MNIST('./data', train=True, download=True, transform=transforms.ToTensor()), batch_size=128, shuffle=True)


# Training loop
model.train()
for epoch in range(1, 11):  # Train for 10 epochs
    train_loss = 0
    for batch_idx, (data, _) in enumerate(train_loader):
        data = data.to(torch.device("cuda")) # Move input data to GPU if available
        optimizer.zero_grad()
        recon_batch, mu, logvar = model(data)
        loss = loss_function(recon_batch, data, mu, logvar)
        loss.backward()
        train_loss += loss.item()
        optimizer.step()

    print(f'Epoch {epoch}, Loss: {train_loss / len(train_loader.dataset)}')
```

In this code:

- **Encoder**: The input image is passed through a fully connected layer that maps it to a latent distribution (mean and log-variance).
- **Reparameterization Trick**: This step ensures that the model is differentiable by sampling from the latent distribution using the mean and log-variance.
- **Decoder**: The sampled latent vector is passed through a decoder that generates the output image.
- **Loss**: The loss is a combination of the **reconstruction loss** and the **KL divergence**.

VAEs are used in various applications, including:

- **Image Generation**: VAEs can generate new images by sampling from the latent space.
- **Data Augmentation**: Generating synthetic data samples to augment the training set.
- **Anomaly Detection**: Using the reconstruction error from a VAE to identify unusual data points.
- **Semi-Supervised Learning**: Leveraging VAEs for unsupervised learning and fine-tuning on labeled data.

9.2. Generative Adversarial Networks (GANs)

A **Generative Adversarial Network (GAN)** is another powerful generative model, introduced by Ian Goodfellow in 2014. GANs consist of two networks: a **generator** and a **discriminator**. The generator tries to create realistic data, while the discriminator tries to distinguish between real data and fake data generated by the generator. The two networks are trained simultaneously in a **game-theoretic** framework, where the generator aims to fool the discriminator, and the discriminator aims to correctly classify real and generated data.

- **Generator**: Takes a random noise vector as input and generates fake data (e.g., images).
- **Discriminator**: Takes both real and fake data as input and classifies whether the data is real or generated.

The generator and discriminator are both trained using a min-max optimization process. The loss for the generator is the negative log-likelihood of the discriminator classifying fake data as real, while the discriminator's loss is the binary cross-entropy between real and fake data.

The overall GAN objective is:

$$\min_G \max_D E_{x \sim p_{data}}[\log D(x)] + E_{z \sim p_z}[\log(1 - D(G(z)))]$$
$$G\min D\max E_{x \sim p_{data}}[\log D(x)] + E_{z \sim p_z}[\log(1 - D(G(z)))]$$

Where:

- $p_{data}p_{data}$ is the distribution of real data,
- $p_z p_z$ is the distribution of noise (input to the generator),
- GG is the generator,
- DD is the discriminator.

Here's how we can implement a basic GAN in PyTorch for generating images.

python
Copy code

```python
class Generator(nn.Module):
    def __init__(self, z_dim):
        super(Generator, self).__init__()
        self.fc = nn.Sequential(
            nn.Linear(z_dim, 128),
            nn.ReLU(True),
            nn.Linear(128, 256),
            nn.ReLU(True),
```

```python
            nn.Linear(256, 512),
            nn.ReLU(True),
            nn.Linear(512, 28 * 28),
            nn.Tanh()
        )

    def forward(self, z):
        return self.fc(z).view(-1, 28, 28)

class Discriminator(nn.Module):
    def __init__(self):
        super(Discriminator, self).__init__()
        self.fc = nn.Sequential(
            nn.Linear(28 * 28, 512),
            nn.LeakyReLU(0.2),
            nn.Linear(512, 256),
            nn.LeakyReLU(0.2),
            nn.Linear(256, 1),
            nn.Sigmoid()
        )

    def forward(self, x):
        return self.fc(x.view(-1, 28 * 28))

# Example usage
z_dim = 100  # Latent space dimension
generator = Generator(z_dim)
discriminator = Discriminator()

# Optimizers
```

```
optimizer_G = optim.Adam(generator.parameters(),
lr=0.0002, betas=(0.5, 0.999))
optimizer_D = optim.Adam(discriminator.parameters(),
lr=0.0002, betas=(0.5, 0.999))
```

In this code:

- The **Generator** network takes random noise (z) and transforms it into a generated image.
- The **Discriminator** network takes an image (real or fake) and classifies it as real or fake.

- **DCGANs (Deep Convolutional GANs)**: A variant of GANs that uses convolutional layers in both the generator and discriminator networks. DCGANs are widely used for image generation because they utilize the spatial structure of images.
- **WGANs (Wasserstein GANs)**: An improvement over standard GANs that use the **Wasserstein distance** as the objective function. WGANs stabilize training and improve the quality of generated samples.

GANs have achieved state-of-the-art results in various domains, including:

- **Image Generation**: GANs can generate high-quality images that are indistinguishable from real ones (e.g., generating new faces).
- **Style Transfer**: GANs can be used for tasks like turning photographs into artistic paintings (e.g., converting an image into the style of Van Gogh).
- **Super-Resolution**: Enhancing the resolution of images by generating high-resolution images from low-resolution inputs.
- **Data Augmentation**: GANs can generate synthetic data to augment datasets, especially in domains where labeled data is scarce.

In this chapter, we explored **Generative Models**, focusing on **Variational Autoencoders (VAEs)** and **Generative Adversarial Networks (GANs)**. We discussed the theory behind VAEs and GANs, walked through the process of implementing them in PyTorch, and explored their applications in areas such as image generation, style transfer, and data augmentation. By mastering these generative models, you can create powerful systems capable of generating realistic data in a variety of domains.

Part 4

Advanced Topics and Techniques

Chapter 10: Reinforcement Learning (RL)

Reinforcement Learning (RL) is an area of machine learning concerned with how agents should take actions in an environment in order to maximize some notion of cumulative reward. Unlike supervised learning, where the model is provided with labeled data, RL agents learn by interacting with their environment and receiving feedback in the form of rewards or penalties. RL has been successfully applied to many complex tasks, including game playing, robotics, and autonomous driving.

In this chapter, we will explore the fundamentals of Reinforcement Learning, covering essential concepts such as **Markov Decision Processes (MDPs)**, **Q-Learning**, **Deep Q-Networks (DQNs)**, **Policy Gradient Methods**, **Actor-Critic Models**, and how to implement RL algorithms in **PyTorch**. Finally, we will touch on **Multi-Agent Reinforcement Learning**, which deals with environments where multiple agents interact.

10.1. Introduction to RL

Reinforcement Learning involves an agent that interacts with an environment to learn how to achieve a specific goal. The goal is typically defined by maximizing a cumulative reward over time. The agent chooses actions based on its current state, receives feedback (reward or penalty), and updates its strategy to improve future decisions.

Key Components of RL:

1. **Agent**: The learner or decision maker that takes actions in an environment.
2. **Environment**: The external system that the agent interacts with.

3. **State (s)**: A representation of the current situation of the agent within the environment.
4. **Action (a)**: A decision or move made by the agent.
5. **Reward (r)**: The feedback signal received after an action is taken, guiding the agent's future actions.
6. **Policy (π)**: A strategy that defines the agent's actions at each state.
7. **Value Function (V)**: A prediction of the future reward an agent can expect from each state.
8. **Q-Function (Q)**: A function that estimates the quality of an action taken in a particular state.

10.2. Markov Decision Processes (MDPs)

A **Markov Decision Process (MDP)** is the mathematical framework used to describe the environment in RL. An MDP is defined by the following components:

- **States (S)**: The set of all possible states the agent can be in.
- **Actions (A)**: The set of all possible actions the agent can take.
- **Transition Probability (P(s' | s, a))**: The probability of moving to state s's' given the current state ss and action aa.
- **Reward Function (R(s, a))**: The immediate reward received after performing action aa in state ss.
- **Discount Factor (γ)**: A factor that discounts future rewards, representing the agent's preference for immediate rewards over future ones.

The objective of the agent in an MDP is to find a policy that maximizes the expected cumulative reward over time, which is typically represented by:

$$\text{Objective} = \max_{\pi} E\left[\sum_{t=0}^{\infty} \gamma^t R(s_t, a_t)\right]$$

Where γγ is the discount factor that balances long-term and short-term rewards.

10.3. Q-Learning and Deep Q-Networks (DQNs)

Q-Learning is a model-free reinforcement learning algorithm that estimates the optimal action-value function, denoted as $Q(s,a)Q(s,a)$. The Q-value represents the expected cumulative reward of taking action aa in state ss and following the optimal policy thereafter.

Deep Q-Networks (DQNs):

In standard Q-Learning, the Q-values are stored in a table, but for large state spaces, this becomes impractical. **Deep Q-Networks (DQNs)** use a deep neural network to approximate the Q-value function, allowing the agent to handle large state spaces and learn from raw data, such as images.

Code Example: Implementing DQN in PyTorch
python
Copy code

```python
import torch
import torch.nn as nn
import torch.optim as optim
import random
import numpy as np
from collections import deque

class DQN(nn.Module):
    def __init__(self, input_dim, output_dim):
        super(DQN, self).__init__()
        self.fc1 = nn.Linear(input_dim, 128)
        self.fc2 = nn.Linear(128, 128)
```

103

```python
        self.fc3 = nn.Linear(128, output_dim)


    def forward(self, x):
        x = torch.relu(self.fc1(x))
        x = torch.relu(self.fc2(x))
        return self.fc3(x)


class DQNAgent:
    def __init__(self, input_dim, output_dim):
        self.model = DQN(input_dim, output_dim)
        self.target_model = DQN(input_dim, output_dim)
        self.optimizer = optim.Adam(self.model.parameters(),
lr=0.001)
        self.memory = deque(maxlen=10000)
        self.batch_size = 64
        self.gamma = 0.99
        self.epsilon = 0.1
        self.target_update_freq = 10


    def store_experience(self, state, action, reward,
next_state, done):
        self.memory.append((state, action, reward, next_state,
done))


    def select_action(self, state):
        if random.random() < self.epsilon:
            return
random.choice(range(self.model.fc3.out_features))  #
Random action
        state = torch.FloatTensor(state).unsqueeze(0)
        q_values = self.model(state)
```

```python
        return torch.argmax(q_values).item()  # Action with
the highest Q-value

    def train(self):
        if len(self.memory) < self.batch_size:
            return

        batch = random.sample(self.memory, self.batch_size)
        states, actions, rewards, next_states, dones =
zip(*batch)

        states = torch.FloatTensor(states)
        actions = torch.LongTensor(actions)
        rewards = torch.FloatTensor(rewards)
        next_states = torch.FloatTensor(next_states)
        dones = torch.FloatTensor(dones)

        # Compute target Q-values
        with torch.no_grad():
            next_q_values = self.target_model(next_states)
            max_next_q_values = next_q_values.max(1)[0]
            target_q_values = rewards + self.gamma *
max_next_q_values * (1 - dones)

        # Compute Q-values
        q_values = self.model(states)
        q_value = q_values.gather(1,
actions.unsqueeze(1)).squeeze(1)

        # Compute loss
```

```python
        loss = nn.MSELoss()(q_value, target_q_values)

        # Backpropagate
        self.optimizer.zero_grad()
        loss.backward()
        self.optimizer.step()

    def update_target_model(self):

self.target_model.load_state_dict(self.model.state_dict())

# Example usage
input_dim = 4  # Example state space (e.g., for CartPole)
output_dim = 2  # Example action space (e.g., left or right)

agent = DQNAgent(input_dim, output_dim)
```

In this implementation:

- The **DQN** class defines the neural network for approximating the Q-values.
- The **DQNAgent** class stores experiences in a memory buffer and updates the Q-values using the Bellman equation.
- The **train** method performs a training step by sampling from the memory, calculating the loss, and updating the network weights.

10.4. Policy Gradient Methods

Policy Gradient Methods are a class of reinforcement learning algorithms that learn the policy directly by optimizing the parameters of the policy network. Unlike Q-Learning, which learns a value function and derives the policy from it, policy gradient methods parameterize the policy using a neural network and optimize the policy directly using gradient ascent.

The key idea is to maximize the expected return using the following objective function:

$$J(\theta)=E\pi[\textstyle\sum t\gamma tRt]J(\theta)=E\pi[t\textstyle\sum\gamma tRt]$$

Where:

- $\theta\theta$ are the parameters of the policy network,
- $\gamma\gamma$ is the discount factor, and
- $RtRt$ is the reward at time step tt.

Policy gradients are computed using the **REINFORCE algorithm**, where the policy is updated using the gradient of the log-probability of the action taken weighted by the total reward.

10.5. Actor-Critic Models

Actor-Critic Models combine the benefits of value-based and policy-based methods. The **actor** updates the policy, while the **critic** evaluates the actions taken by the actor by estimating the value function. The actor selects actions based on the policy, and the critic provides feedback by computing the value function of the current state.

The key advantage of actor-critic models is that the critic can reduce the variance of the policy gradient estimates, making training more stable and efficient.

10.6. Implementing RL Algorithms in PyTorch

Implementing RL algorithms in PyTorch is straightforward thanks to the flexibility of the framework. In this section, we have already covered some basic implementations of **Q-Learning**, **DQNs**, and policy gradient methods. PyTorch provides automatic differentiation, which makes it easy to compute gradients for backpropagation, even in the complex environments typically used in RL.

10.7. Multi-Agent Reinforcement Learning

In **Multi-Agent Reinforcement Learning (MARL)**, multiple agents interact with the environment and with each other. This setting is relevant for tasks such as **robotics**, **autonomous driving**, and **game playing**.

Each agent in MARL has its own policy, but the agents need to learn how to cooperate or compete based on the environment and each other's actions. MARL introduces additional challenges, such as **non-stationarity** (since the environment changes due to other agents' actions), and requires methods for communication and coordination.

Some popular MARL approaches include:

- **Independent Q-Learning**: Each agent independently learns its own Q-function and updates its policy.
- **Cooperative MARL**: Agents collaborate by sharing rewards or actions to achieve a common goal.

In this chapter, we introduced the fundamentals of **Reinforcement Learning (RL)**, covering the core concepts such as **Markov Decision Processes (MDPs)**, **Q-Learning**, **Deep Q-Networks (DQNs)**, **Policy Gradient Methods**, and **Actor-Critic Models**. We also discussed how to implement RL algorithms in **PyTorch** and explored the growing field of **Multi-Agent Reinforcement Learning (MARL)**. RL has wide applications, from game-playing AI to autonomous systems, and understanding these techniques will give you the tools to tackle complex decision-making tasks.

Chapter 11: Optimization and Model Performance

Optimizing machine learning models is crucial for achieving the best performance while ensuring that the model is efficient in terms of both time and computational resources. This chapter will cover several key aspects of model optimization, including hyperparameter tuning, model pruning and quantization, distributed training with PyTorch, and strategies for optimizing inference with a focus on balancing latency and throughput.

11.1. Hyperparameter Tuning

Hyperparameter tuning is the process of finding the best set of hyperparameters for a given model. Hyperparameters are parameters that are not learned from the data but set manually, such as the learning rate, batch size, number of layers, and units per layer. Optimizing hyperparameters is essential because they can significantly affect model performance. In this section, we will discuss three popular hyperparameter optimization methods: Grid Search, Random Search, and Bayesian Optimization.

- Grid Search: Grid search is a brute-force method for hyperparameter optimization. It systematically searches through a manually defined hyperparameter space by evaluating every possible combination of hyperparameters. Although grid search guarantees that the best combination within the grid will be found, it can be computationally expensive and time-consuming, especially when the hyperparameter space is large.

Code Example: Grid Search in PyTorch

python

Copy code

```python
from sklearn.model_selection import GridSearchCV

import torch

import torch.nn as nn

import torch.optim as optim

from sklearn.datasets import load_iris

from sklearn.model_selection import train_test_split


# Example neural network model
class SimpleNN(nn.Module):
    def __init__(self, hidden_layer_size):
        super(SimpleNN, self).__init__()
        self.fc1 = nn.Linear(4, hidden_layer_size)
        self.fc2 = nn.Linear(hidden_layer_size, 3)  # Iris has 3 classes

    def forward(self, x):
        x = torch.relu(self.fc1(x))
        return self.fc2(x)


# Sample data (Iris dataset)
data = load_iris()
```

```python
X = data.data

y = data.target

X_train, X_test, y_train, y_test = train_test_split(X, y,
test_size=0.2)


# Defining the hyperparameter grid

param_grid = {'hidden_layer_size': [10, 20, 30],
'batch_size': [16, 32]}


# Grid search implementation (dummy example)

for hidden_layer_size in param_grid['hidden_layer_size']:

    for batch_size in param_grid['batch_size']:

      model =
SimpleNN(hidden_layer_size=hidden_layer_size)

      optimizer = optim.SGD(model.parameters(), lr=0.01)

      criterion = nn.CrossEntropyLoss()

      # Train the model with current hyperparameters (not
fully implemented)

      # Evaluate the model's performance on validation/test
set

      print(f"Training with
hidden_layer_size={hidden_layer_size},
batch_size={batch_size}")
```

In this example:

- We perform grid search over two hyperparameters: hidden_layer_size and batch_size for the neural network model. The training process is simplified, but in a real-world scenario, you would evaluate the performance on the validation set.
- Random Search: Random search is another method for hyperparameter optimization. Instead of searching every possible combination, random search randomly samples from the hyperparameter space. It is more efficient than grid search when the hyperparameter space is large, as it can potentially find better combinations in fewer trials.

Code Example: Random Search

python

Copy code

```python
from sklearn.model_selection import RandomizedSearchCV

import numpy as np


# Define the parameter distribution

param_dist = {'hidden_layer_size': np.arange(10, 50, 10), 'batch_size': [16, 32, 64]}


# Randomized search implementation (dummy example)

for hidden_layer_size in np.random.choice(param_dist['hidden_layer_size'], size=3):
```

```python
    for batch_size in
np.random.choice(param_dist['batch_size'], size=3):

        model =
SimpleNN(hidden_layer_size=hidden_layer_size)

        optimizer = optim.SGD(model.parameters(), lr=0.01)

        criterion = nn.CrossEntropyLoss()

        # Train the model with current hyperparameters (not
fully implemented)

        # Evaluate the model's performance

        print(f"Training with
hidden_layer_size={hidden_layer_size},
batch_size={batch_size}")
```

Here, we use random sampling instead of searching all combinations, which can be more efficient for larger hyperparameter spaces.

Bayesian optimization is a more sophisticated approach for hyperparameter tuning. Unlike grid and random search, Bayesian optimization models the objective function (e.g., model accuracy) as a probabilistic model and uses this model to select the next set of hyperparameters to try. It balances exploration (trying new areas) and exploitation (focusing on the most promising areas based on past evaluations).

Bayesian optimization is typically implemented using libraries like Optuna or Hyperopt. The key advantage of Bayesian optimization is that it can find good hyperparameters more efficiently by reducing the number of trials.

11.2. Model Pruning and Quantization

Model pruning and quantization are techniques used to optimize a trained model for inference, reducing its size and improving its speed without significantly compromising accuracy.

Model Pruning

Pruning involves removing unnecessary or less important weights (or neurons) from the model. The idea is that not all weights contribute equally to the model's performance, so pruning can help reduce the model's size and computational cost.

Code Example: Model Pruning in PyTorch

python

Copy code

```
import torch.nn.utils.prune as prune


# Example of pruning a fully connected layer

model = SimpleNN(hidden_layer_size=20)

prune.random_unstructured(model.fc1, name="weight",
amount=0.3)  # Prune 30% of weights


# Check the pruning

print(model.fc1.weight)
```

In this example:

- We apply random unstructured pruning, which removes a random 30% of the weights in the first fully connected layer (fc1).

Model Quantization

Quantization involves reducing the precision of the model's weights and activations from floating-point (32-bit) to lower precision formats like INT8 or FP16. This helps reduce memory usage and speeds up inference on specialized hardware, such as mobile devices or edge devices.

Code Example: Quantization in PyTorch

python

Copy code

```python
import torch.quantization


# Example of quantizing a model

model = SimpleNN(hidden_layer_size=20)


# Convert model to quantized version

model = torch.quantization.quantize_dynamic(model,
{nn.Linear}, dtype=torch.qint8)


# Check the quantized model

print(model)
```

Here:

- We apply dynamic quantization to the Linear layers of the model. This reduces the precision of the weights, making the model more efficient for inference.

11.3. Distributed Training with PyTorch

For large-scale machine learning tasks, distributed training allows models to be trained across multiple devices (e.g., GPUs) or even across multiple nodes in a network. PyTorch provides robust support for distributed training using DistributedDataParallel (DDP).

Example: Distributed Training in PyTorch

python

Copy code

```python
import torch

import torch.nn as nn

import torch.optim as optim

import torch.distributed as dist

from torch.nn.parallel import DistributedDataParallel as DDP


def setup(rank, world_size):
    dist.init_process_group("nccl", rank=rank,
world_size=world_size)
```

```python
def cleanup():
    dist.destroy_process_group()


class SimpleNN(nn.Module):
    def __init__(self):
        super(SimpleNN, self).__init__()
        self.fc = nn.Linear(10, 10)

    def forward(self, x):
        return self.fc(x)


def train(rank, world_size):
    setup(rank, world_size)
    model = SimpleNN().to(rank)
    model = DDP(model, device_ids=[rank])

    optimizer = optim.SGD(model.parameters(), lr=0.01)
    criterion = nn.CrossEntropyLoss()

    # Training loop
    for epoch in range(10):
```

```python
        optimizer.zero_grad()

        output = model(torch.randn(10, 10).to(rank))

        target = torch.randint(0, 10, (10,)).to(rank)

        loss = criterion(output, target)

        loss.backward()

        optimizer.step()

        print(f"Rank {rank}, Epoch {epoch}, Loss {loss.item()}")


    cleanup()


# Assuming we have 2 GPUs, we run this across 2 processes
from torch.multiprocessing import Process


world_size = 2
processes = []


for rank in range(world_size):
    p = Process(target=train, args=(rank, world_size))
    p.start()
    processes.append(p)
```

```
for p in processes:

  p.join()
```

In this code:

- We use DistributedDataParallel to parallelize the model across two devices (GPUs). This allows us to train the model faster by distributing the workload.
- The init_process_group function initializes the distributed training environment.

11.4. Optimizing for Inference (Latency vs. Throughput)

When deploying models to production, it's important to consider the trade-off between latency and throughput. Latencyrefers to the time it takes to process a single input, while throughput refers to the number of inputs processed per unit of time.

To optimize for inference, several techniques can be used:

- Batching: Process multiple inputs at once (batch processing) to improve throughput.
- Model Simplification: Use techniques like pruning and quantization to simplify the model and reduce inference time.
- Hardware Acceleration: Use specialized hardware like TPUs or FPGAs for faster processing.

Balancing Latency and Throughput

- For applications where real-time predictions are crucial (e.g., online recommendation systems, autonomous driving), low latency is critical, and you may sacrifice throughput for faster response times.

- For batch processing tasks (e.g., training, bulk predictions), throughput is more important, and batching inputs together can maximize efficiency.

In this chapter, we explored the essential techniques for optimizing machine learning models, including hyperparameter tuning methods like grid search, random search, and Bayesian optimization. We discussed how to improve model performance through model pruning and quantization. Additionally, we covered the importance of distributed trainingwith PyTorch for large-scale models, and strategies for optimizing inference with a focus on balancing latency and throughput. These optimization techniques help you deploy models that are efficient, scalable, and suitable for production environments.

In the next chapter, we will delve into deployment strategies for machine learning models, focusing on how to serve models in real-time applications and optimize them for production systems.

Chapter 12: Model Deployment

Once a machine learning model is trained and optimized, the next crucial step is deployment. Deploying models efficiently ensures that they can be used to make predictions in real-world applications. This chapter will cover several methods of deploying PyTorch models, ranging from exporting models for different environments, serving models via APIs, and deploying models on cloud platforms and edge devices. We will focus on the following key topics: saving and exporting PyTorch models, deploying models with PyTorch Serve, exporting to ONNX format, serving models using Flask/Django APIs, deploying on cloud platforms (AWS, GCP, Azure), and edge deployment for mobile inference.

12.1. Saving and Exporting PyTorch Models

Saving and exporting models in PyTorch is essential for model deployment. PyTorch provides flexible options to save and load model weights, allowing you to save the entire model or just the learned parameters.

Saving the Model State Dict

The most common approach is to save the model's state dictionary (state_dict), which contains all the weights and biases of the model. This method allows you to easily load the model later and fine-tune it or use it for inference.

python

Copy code

```
import torch
import torch.nn as nn
```

```python
# Example model
class SimpleNN(nn.Module):
    def __init__(self):
        super(SimpleNN, self).__init__()
        self.fc = nn.Linear(10, 2)

    def forward(self, x):
        return self.fc(x)


# Instantiate the model
model = SimpleNN()


# Save model weights (state_dict)
torch.save(model.state_dict(), 'simple_nn.pth')


# Load model weights
model = SimpleNN()
model.load_state_dict(torch.load('simple_nn.pth'))
model.eval()  # Set model to evaluation mode
```

In this code:

- We save the model's state dictionary using torch.save().
- We load the state dictionary into a new instance of the model using model.load_state_dict().

Saving the Entire Model

PyTorch also allows you to save the entire model, including both the architecture and weights. However, this is generally less flexible and not recommended for deployment, as it ties the model to the specific code used to define it.

python

Copy code

```
# Save the entire model (including architecture)

torch.save(model, 'simple_nn_full.pth')


# Load the entire model

loaded_model = torch.load('simple_nn_full.pth')

loaded_model.eval()
```

This method saves the entire model object, which makes it easy to load and use directly, but it is less portable and can lead to issues when there are changes in the PyTorch version or code dependencies.

12.2. Deploying Models with PyTorch Serve

PyTorch Serve is a flexible and easy-to-use tool for serving PyTorch models in production. It provides REST APIs for serving models and includes features like multi-model support, batch inference, and logging.

Steps to Deploy with PyTorch Serve

Install PyTorch Serve: Install PyTorch Serve and dependencies by running the following command:

bash

Copy code

```
pip install torchserve torch-model-archiver
```

Prepare the Model: Before deploying a model, you need to archive it into a .mar file. This file contains the model's weights, its configuration, and any required code (e.g., pre-processing or post-processing).

bash

Copy code

```
torch-model-archiver --model-name simple_nn --version
1.0 --serialized-file simple_nn.pth --handler
image_classifier
```

Start PyTorch Serve: Once the model is archived, you can start PyTorch Serve to deploy the model:

bash

Copy code

```
torchserve --start --model-store model_store --models
simple_nn=mar_file.mar
```

Access the Model: After starting PyTorch Serve, you can access the model via HTTP requests (REST APIs). For example, using curl:

bash

Copy code

```
curl -X POST http://127.0.0.1:8080/predictions/simple_nn -
T test_image.jpg
```

This allows you to deploy your model and serve predictions via HTTP, making it easy to integrate with web applications or other services.

12.3. Exporting to ONNX Format

The Open Neural Network Exchange (ONNX) format is a cross-platform framework designed to allow models to be shared and deployed across different environments. ONNX supports models trained in PyTorch, TensorFlow, Scikit-learn, and other machine learning frameworks. Exporting a model to ONNX allows you to run it in environments where PyTorch may not be supported, such as mobile devices or specialized inference engines.

Exporting a PyTorch Model to ONNX

PyTorch provides a simple method to export models to the ONNX format using torch.onnx.export().

python

Copy code

```python
import torch.onnx


# Load a model and set it to evaluation mode

model = SimpleNN()

model.load_state_dict(torch.load('simple_nn.pth'))

model.eval()
```

```
# Example input tensor (e.g., for image classification)

x = torch.randn(1, 10)


# Export the model to ONNX

torch.onnx.export(model, x, "simple_nn.onnx",
verbose=True)
```

In this example:

- We export the model to simple_nn.onnx, which can then be used in other frameworks like TensorFlow or in inference engines like ONNX Runtime.

Using ONNX for Inference

Once the model is exported to ONNX, you can load it in any platform that supports ONNX, including mobile devices and edge devices, using tools like ONNX Runtime or TensorFlow Lite.

12.4. Serving PyTorch Models with Flask/Django APIs

For web applications, serving a PyTorch model via a REST API is common. You can use frameworks like Flask or Django to serve models and handle HTTP requests for predictions.

Serving a PyTorch Model with Flask

Flask is a lightweight framework that can be used to create simple REST APIs for serving models.

python

Copy code

```python
from flask import Flask, request, jsonify
import torch
import torch.nn as nn
import numpy as np

app = Flask(__name__)

# Define the model (same as before)
class SimpleNN(nn.Module):
    def __init__(self):
        super(SimpleNN, self).__init__()
        self.fc = nn.Linear(10, 2)

    def forward(self, x):
        return self.fc(x)

# Load the trained model
model = SimpleNN()
model.load_state_dict(torch.load('simple_nn.pth'))
```

```python
model.eval()

@app.route('/predict', methods=['POST'])
def predict():
    # Get the input data from the request
    data = request.get_json()
    input_data = np.array(data['input'])

    # Convert to tensor
    input_tensor = torch.FloatTensor(input_data)

    # Make prediction
    with torch.no_grad():
        output = model(input_tensor)

    # Return the result
    return jsonify({'output': output.tolist()})

if __name__ == '__main__':
    app.run(debug=True)
```

In this example:

- A Flask app serves the trained model at the /predict endpoint.
- The model takes input from a JSON payload, processes it, and returns predictions in the response.

You can deploy this API to a server (e.g., using gunicorn for production deployment) and integrate it into any web or mobile application that needs access to the model.

12.5. Deploying Models on Cloud Platforms (AWS, GCP, Azure)

Deploying models on cloud platforms like Amazon Web Services (AWS), Google Cloud Platform (GCP), and Microsoft Azure allows you to scale the inference capabilities and integrate with other cloud services.

AWS SageMaker

Amazon SageMaker is a fully managed service for building, training, and deploying machine learning models. You can easily deploy PyTorch models on SageMaker by using pre-built containers for PyTorch.

1. Create a Model: You first upload the model to Amazon S3.
2. Deploy the Model: Use SageMaker's built-in deployment options to deploy the model as a REST API endpoint.

python

Copy code

```python
import sagemaker

from sagemaker.pytorch import PyTorchModel
```

```
# Define the model

model =
PyTorchModel(model_data='s3://path/to/model.tar.gz',
role='arn:aws:iam::account-id:role/role-name')
```

```
# Deploy the model

predictor = model.deploy(instance_type='ml.m5.large',
initial_instance_count=1)
```

GCP AI Platform

Google Cloud AI Platform allows you to deploy PyTorch models using the TensorFlow Serving container or GCP's custom containers.

1. Upload the Model to GCP Storage: Store your model on Google Cloud Storage (GCS).
2. Deploy the Model: Use AI Platform to deploy the model.

bash

Copy code

```
gcloud ai-platform models create my_model --regions=us-central1

gcloud ai-platform versions create v1 --model=my_model --origin=gs://path/to/model
```

Azure Machine Learning

Azure provides a similar experience to AWS and GCP, offering services like Azure ML to deploy models with ease.

1. Register the Model: Upload the model to Azure Blob Storage.
2. Deploy the Model: Create a container and deploy the model.

python

Copy code

```python
from azureml.core import Workspace, Model


ws = Workspace.from_config()


model = Model.register(workspace=ws, model_name="simple_nn", model_path="simple_nn.pth")
```

12.6. Edge Deployment and Mobile Inference

For deploying models on edge devices or mobile platforms, PyTorch provides PyTorch Mobile, which allows you to run PyTorch models on mobile devices (both Android and iOS). This is especially useful for applications that require low latency or offline predictions.

Using PyTorch Mobile

1. Optimize the Model: Before deploying on mobile, it's often useful to optimize the model for performance (e.g., using quantization).
2. Export to TorchScript: You can export the model to TorchScript, which is a serialized representation of the model that can be loaded and run on mobile.

python

Copy code

```python
import torch

# Example of exporting a model for mobile
model = SimpleNN()
model.load_state_dict(torch.load('simple_nn.pth'))
model.eval()

# Convert to TorchScript
scripted_model = torch.jit.script(model)
scripted_model.save('simple_nn_mobile.pt')
```

This saved model can be used in mobile apps with PyTorch Mobile.

In this chapter, we explored various strategies for deploying PyTorch models in real-world applications. We covered methods for saving and exporting models, deploying with PyTorch Serve, exporting to the ONNX format, and using Flask/Django for serving models through APIs. We also discussed deploying models on cloud platforms such as AWS, GCP, and Azure, and deploying on edge devices and mobile using PyTorch Mobile. Understanding these deployment strategies will enable you to integrate machine learning models into production systems efficiently and effectively.

Part 5

Practical Deep Learning Projects

Chapter 13: Image Classification with CNNs

Image classification is one of the most common applications of deep learning, and Convolutional Neural Networks (CNNs) are the backbone of most state-of-the-art image classification models. In this chapter, we will explore how to build and train a CNN for image classification tasks. We will also cover dataset preparation (using popular datasets like CIFAR-10 and MNIST), model evaluation, and deployment to the web.

13.1. Dataset Preparation (CIFAR-10, MNIST)

Before we can train a model for image classification, we need to prepare the dataset. A good dataset is essential for training a model that can generalize well. We will use two widely used image datasets in this chapter:

- CIFAR-10: A dataset containing 60,000 32x32 color images in 10 classes, with 6,000 images per class. These images are categorized into 10 classes, such as airplane, automobile, bird, cat, dog, etc.
- MNIST: A dataset of handwritten digits (0–9). It consists of 60,000 training images and 10,000 testing images, each of size 28x28 pixels.

Loading the Dataset in PyTorch

PyTorch provides an easy way to load datasets using the torchvision library, which provides utilities for loading common datasets like CIFAR-10 and MNIST.

python

Copy code

```python
import torch

import torchvision

import torchvision.transforms as transforms

from torch.utils.data import DataLoader


# Define the transformations to apply to the data (e.g., normalization)

transform = transforms.Compose([

    transforms.ToTensor(),  # Convert images to tensor

    transforms.Normalize(mean=[0.5, 0.5, 0.5], std=[0.5, 0.5, 0.5])  # Normalize with mean and std

])


# CIFAR-10 dataset

trainset = torchvision.datasets.CIFAR10(root='./data', train=True, download=True, transform=transform)

testset = torchvision.datasets.CIFAR10(root='./data', train=False, download=True, transform=transform)


trainloader = DataLoader(trainset, batch_size=64, shuffle=True)

testloader = DataLoader(testset, batch_size=64, shuffle=False)
```

In the code above:

- We load the CIFAR-10 dataset using torchvision.datasets.CIFAR10().
- We apply a transformation to normalize the images and convert them to PyTorch tensors.
- We create DataLoader objects to handle batching and shuffling.

You can similarly load the MNIST dataset by replacing CIFAR10 with MNIST.

python

Copy code

```python
# MNIST dataset

trainset_mnist = torchvision.datasets.MNIST(root='./data', train=True, download=True, transform=transform)

testset_mnist = torchvision.datasets.MNIST(root='./data', train=False, download=True, transform=transform)


trainloader_mnist = DataLoader(trainset_mnist, batch_size=64, shuffle=True)

testloader_mnist = DataLoader(testset_mnist, batch_size=64, shuffle=False)
```

13.2. Building and Training a CNN for Classification

Now that we have the dataset, we can start building and training the Convolutional Neural Network (CNN). CNNs are highly effective for image classification tasks because they are designed to capture spatial hierarchies in images through convolution operations.

Building the CNN Model

A basic CNN model consists of several convolutional layers, followed by pooling layers, and fully connected layers. Here's a simple architecture for image classification using CIFAR-10 or MNIST:

python

Copy code

```python
import torch.nn as nn

import torch.optim as optim


# Define the CNN model

class SimpleCNN(nn.Module):

    def __init__(self):

        super(SimpleCNN, self).__init__()


        # Convolutional layer 1: 3 channels (RGB) -> 32 filters of size 3x3

        self.conv1 = nn.Conv2d(3, 32, kernel_size=3, padding=1)

        self.pool = nn.MaxPool2d(2, 2)  # Max pooling layer with 2x2 window


        # Convolutional layer 2: 32 filters -> 64 filters
```

```python
        self.conv2 = nn.Conv2d(32, 64, kernel_size=3,
padding=1)


    # Fully connected layer 1

        self.fc1 = nn.Linear(64 * 8 * 8, 512)  # Flattened to 64 * 8
* 8 after pooling

        self.fc2 = nn.Linear(512, 10)  # Output 10 classes (for
CIFAR-10)


    def forward(self, x):
        # Apply convolution, ReLU activation, and max pooling

        x = self.pool(torch.relu(self.conv1(x)))

        x = self.pool(torch.relu(self.conv2(x)))


        # Flatten the output from the convolutional layers

        x = x.view(-1, 64 * 8 * 8)


        # Fully connected layers

        x = torch.relu(self.fc1(x))

        x = self.fc2(x)  # Output raw scores for 10 classes

        return x
```

```python
# Instantiate the model

model = SimpleCNN()
```

Training the CNN

Now that we have the model, we can proceed to the training phase. This involves defining the loss function, optimizer, and training loop.

python

Copy code

```python
# Define the loss function (CrossEntropyLoss for classification)

criterion = nn.CrossEntropyLoss()


# Define the optimizer (Stochastic Gradient Descent)

optimizer = optim.SGD(model.parameters(), lr=0.001, momentum=0.9)


# Training loop

for epoch in range(10):  # Loop over the dataset multiple times
    running_loss = 0.0
    for i, data in enumerate(trainloader, 0):
        inputs, labels = data

        optimizer.zero_grad()  # Zero the parameter gradients
```

```python
# Forward pass
outputs = model(inputs)

# Compute loss
loss = criterion(outputs, labels)

# Backward pass and optimization
loss.backward()
optimizer.step()

running_loss += loss.item()
if i % 100 == 99:  # Print every 100 mini-batches
    print(f"[{epoch + 1}, {i + 1:5d}] loss: {running_loss / 100:.3f}")
    running_loss = 0.0

print('Finished Training')
```

In this training loop:

- We use CrossEntropyLoss, which is a commonly used loss function for classification tasks.

- We optimize the model using Stochastic Gradient Descent (SGD) with momentum.
- The model is trained for 10 epochs, with the loss printed every 100 mini-batches.

13.3. Model Evaluation and Metrics

After training the model, the next step is to evaluate its performance. This can be done by testing the model on a separate test set and calculating metrics like accuracy, precision, recall, and F1 score.

Evaluating the Model

python

Copy code

```python
# Model evaluation

correct = 0

total = 0

with torch.no_grad():  # No need to compute gradients during inference

    for data in testloader:

        inputs, labels = data

        outputs = model(inputs)


        # Get the predicted class

        _, predicted = torch.max(outputs, 1)

        total += labels.size(0)
```

```python
    correct += (predicted == labels).sum().item()


# Print accuracy

accuracy = 100 * correct / total

print(f"Accuracy on test set: {accuracy:.2f}%")
```

This code calculates the accuracy of the model by comparing the predicted class with the true labels in the test set.

Other Metrics

You may also want to calculate additional evaluation metrics, such as precision, recall, and F1 score, to gain deeper insights into your model's performance.

python

Copy code

```python
from sklearn.metrics import classification_report


# Get all predictions and true labels for further analysis

y_true = []

y_pred = []


with torch.no_grad():

    for data in testloader:
```

```
    inputs, labels = data

    outputs = model(inputs)

    _, predicted = torch.max(outputs, 1)

    y_true.extend(labels.numpy())

    y_pred.extend(predicted.numpy())


# Generate a classification report

print(classification_report(y_true, y_pred))
```

The classification report gives detailed performance metrics, including precision, recall, and F1 score for each class.

13.4. Model Deployment to the Web

Once the model is trained and evaluated, we can deploy it to the web to make it accessible for real-time predictions. We can use Flask or Django to build a web service that serves the model through a REST API.

Deploying with Flask

Here's a simple Flask application that serves the trained CNN model for inference via HTTP requests.

python

Copy code

```
from flask import Flask, request, jsonify
```

```python
import torch
from torchvision import transforms
from PIL import Image
import io


app = Flask(__name__)


# Load the trained model
model = SimpleCNN()
model.load_state_dict(torch.load('simple_nn.pth'))
model.eval()


# Define transformation for incoming images
transform = transforms.Compose([
    transforms.Resize((32, 32)),  # Resize to CIFAR-10 size
    transforms.ToTensor(),
    transforms.Normalize(mean=[0.5, 0.5, 0.5], std=[0.5, 0.5,
0.5])
])


@app.route('/predict', methods=['POST'])
def predict():
```

```python
    # Get the image from the request

    img_file = request.files['image']

    img = Image.open(io.BytesIO(img_file.read()))


    # Preprocess the image

    img = transform(img).unsqueeze(0)  # Add batch
dimension


    # Make prediction

    with torch.no_grad():

        output = model(img)

        _, predicted = torch.max(output, 1)


    return jsonify({'prediction': predicted.item()})


if __name__ == '__main__':

    app.run(debug=True)
```

In this Flask app:

- The model is loaded, and a transformation is applied to the incoming image before making predictions.
- The app expects a POST request with an image, processes it, and returns the predicted class.

To deploy this Flask app in production, you can use a web server like Gunicorn or uWSGI and deploy it to cloud platforms or servers.

In this chapter, we covered the essentials of image classification with CNNs, from dataset preparation using CIFAR-10and MNIST to building, training, and evaluating a simple CNN model. We also discussed how to deploy the model for real-time inference using Flask. By understanding these concepts and steps, you can build and deploy image classification models effectively for a variety of use cases, from research to production systems. In the next chapter, we will explore transfer learning, which allows you to leverage pre-trained models for faster and more efficient training on new tasks.

Chapter 14: Natural Language Processing with RNNs and Transformers

Natural Language Processing (NLP) is a subfield of AI that focuses on the interaction between computers and human (natural) languages. NLP enables machines to read, interpret, and generate human language in a way that is valuable. In this chapter, we will explore how Recurrent Neural Networks (RNNs) and Transformers can be used to tackle various NLP tasks, such as sentiment analysis, named entity recognition (NER), text generation, and building a chatbot. We will focus on the following topics:

1. Sentiment Analysis with LSTMs
2. Named Entity Recognition (NER) with Transformers
3. Text Generation with LSTMs and GPT-2
4. Building a Transformer-based Chatbot

Each section will provide a detailed, step-by-step guide on how to use these models and techniques for different NLP tasks.

14.1. Sentiment Analysis with LSTMs

Sentiment analysis is a common NLP task that involves determining the sentiment of a piece of text, such as whether a review is positive, negative, or neutral. Long Short-Term Memory (LSTM) networks, a type of Recurrent Neural Network (RNN), are well-suited for sequence-based tasks like sentiment analysis due to their ability to capture long-range dependencies in text.

Building an LSTM for Sentiment Analysis

We will use the IMDb movie review dataset for sentiment analysis, which contains 50,000 movie reviews labeled as positive or negative.

Step 1: Dataset Preparation

python

Copy code

```python
import torch

from torch.utils.data import DataLoader

from torchvision import datasets, transforms

from torchtext.datasets import IMDB

from torchtext.data import Field, BucketIterator


# Define fields for processing the text and labels

TEXT = Field(sequential=True, tokenize='spacy',
include_lengths=True)

LABEL = Field(sequential=False, use_vocab=True,
is_target=True)


# Load the IMDB dataset

train_data, test_data = IMDB.splits(TEXT, LABEL)


# Build the vocabulary using GloVe embeddings

TEXT.build_vocab(train_data, vectors='glove.6B.100d',
unk_init=torch.Tensor.normal_)

LABEL.build_vocab(train_data)
```

```python
# Create data iterators for batching

train_iterator, test_iterator =
BucketIterator.splits((train_data, test_data),
batch_size=64, device=torch.device('cuda'))
```

In this code:

- We load the IMDb dataset and prepare the text and labels for training.
- We tokenize the text using spaCy and create a vocabulary with GloVe embeddings.

Step 2: Defining the LSTM Model

python

Copy code

```python
import torch.nn as nn

import torch.optim as optim


class SentimentLSTM(nn.Module):
    def __init__(self, input_dim, embedding_dim,
hidden_dim, output_dim, n_layers, dropout):

        super(SentimentLSTM, self).__init__()

        self.embedding = nn.Embedding(input_dim,
embedding_dim)

        self.lstm = nn.LSTM(embedding_dim, hidden_dim,
num_layers=n_layers, dropout=dropout, batch_first=True)
```

```python
        self.fc = nn.Linear(hidden_dim, output_dim)

        self.dropout = nn.Dropout(dropout)


    def forward(self, text, text_lengths):

        embedded = self.embedding(text)

        packed_embedded =
nn.utils.rnn.pack_padded_sequence(embedded,
text_lengths, batch_first=True, enforce_sorted=False)

        packed_output, (hidden, cell) =
self.lstm(packed_embedded)

        hidden = self.dropout(hidden[-1])

        return self.fc(hidden)


# Initialize the model

input_dim = len(TEXT.vocab)

embedding_dim = 100

hidden_dim = 256

output_dim = 1  # Binary output (positive or negative)

n_layers = 2

dropout = 0.5

model = SentimentLSTM(input_dim, embedding_dim,
hidden_dim, output_dim, n_layers, dropout)
```

Here:

- The LSTM model is defined with an embedding layer for word representations, followed by an LSTM layer, and a fully connected layer to output the sentiment.
- The model processes text sequences, and the hidden state from the last LSTM layer is used to classify the sentiment.

Step 3: Training the Model

python

Copy code

```python
optimizer = optim.Adam(model.parameters())

criterion = nn.BCEWithLogitsLoss()


# Move model to GPU if available

model = model.to(torch.device('cuda'))

criterion = criterion.to(torch.device('cuda'))


# Training loop

for epoch in range(5):

    model.train()

    for batch in train_iterator:

        text, text_lengths = batch.text

        labels = batch.label

        optimizer.zero_grad()
```

```python
    predictions = model(text, text_lengths).squeeze(1)

    loss = criterion(predictions, labels.float())

    loss.backward()

    optimizer.step()


    print(f"Epoch {epoch+1}, Loss: {loss.item()}")
```

In the training loop:

- We use Binary Cross-Entropy with logits (BCEWithLogitsLoss) since the task is binary classification (positive or negative sentiment).
- The model is trained for 5 epochs, and the loss is printed after each epoch.

Step 4: Model Evaluation

python

Copy code

```python
model.eval()

correct, total = 0, 0

with torch.no_grad():

  for batch in test_iterator:

    text, text_lengths = batch.text

    labels = batch.label

    predictions = model(text, text_lengths).squeeze(1)
```

```python
    predicted_labels =
torch.round(torch.sigmoid(predictions))

    correct += (predicted_labels == labels).sum().item()

    total += labels.size(0)


accuracy = correct / total

print(f"Accuracy on test set: {accuracy:.2f}")
```

The model's performance is evaluated on the test set, and accuracy is computed by comparing the predicted labels with the true labels.

14.2. Named Entity Recognition (NER) with Transformers

Named Entity Recognition (NER) is an NLP task where the goal is to identify entities in text, such as names, dates, and locations. Transformer models, particularly BERT (Bidirectional Encoder Representations from Transformers), have proven highly effective for NER tasks due to their ability to capture contextual relationships in text.

Step 1: Dataset Preparation for NER

We will use the CoNLL-2003 NER dataset, which contains tagged named entities.

python

Copy code

```python
from transformers import BertTokenizer
```

```python
from datasets import load_dataset


# Load the CoNLL-2003 NER dataset

dataset = load_dataset("conll2003")

tokenizer = BertTokenizer.from_pretrained('bert-base-uncased')


def tokenize_and_align_labels(examples):

    tokenized_inputs = tokenizer(examples["tokens"], truncation=True, padding=True, is_split_into_words=True)

    labels = examples["ner_tags"]

    return tokenized_inputs, labels


# Apply the tokenization to the dataset

train_dataset = dataset["train"].map(tokenize_and_align_labels, batched=True)

test_dataset = dataset["test"].map(tokenize_and_align_labels, batched=True)
```

Here:

- We load the CoNLL-2003 dataset using the datasets library.
- We tokenize the text and align the labels for NER.

Step 2: Building the Transformer Model for NER

We will fine-tune a pre-trained BERT model for the NER task using the Hugging Face Transformers library.

python

Copy code

```python
from transformers import BertForTokenClassification, Trainer, TrainingArguments


# Initialize the BERT model for token classification

model = BertForTokenClassification.from_pretrained('bert-base-uncased',
num_labels=len(dataset["train"].features["ner_tags"].feature))


# Define training arguments

training_args = TrainingArguments(

    output_dir="./results",

    num_train_epochs=3,

    per_device_train_batch_size=16,

    per_device_eval_batch_size=64,

    warmup_steps=500,

    weight_decay=0.01,

    logging_dir="./logs",
```

```python
)


# Initialize the Trainer

trainer = Trainer(

    model=model,

    args=training_args,

    train_dataset=train_dataset,

    eval_dataset=test_dataset,

    tokenizer=tokenizer,

)


# Train the model

trainer.train()
```

In this code:

- We use BERT for token classification, which is ideal for NER tasks.
- We fine-tune the model on the CoNLL-2003 dataset using the Trainer API from Hugging Face Transformers.

14.3. Text Generation with LSTMs and GPT-2

Text generation involves creating new text that is similar to the input text. We can use LSTMs or GPT-2 (a transformer-based model) for this task.

Text Generation with LSTMs

LSTMs can be used to generate text character by character or word by word. Here's an example of how to train an LSTM for text generation.

python

Copy code

```python
class TextGeneratorLSTM(nn.Module):

    def __init__(self, vocab_size, embedding_dim, hidden_dim, output_dim):

        super(TextGeneratorLSTM, self).__init__()

        self.embedding = nn.Embedding(vocab_size, embedding_dim)

        self.lstm = nn.LSTM(embedding_dim, hidden_dim, batch_first=True)

        self.fc = nn.Linear(hidden_dim, vocab_size)


    def forward(self, x):

        embedded = self.embedding(x)

        lstm_out, _ = self.lstm(embedded)

        out = self.fc(lstm_out)

        return out
```

```python
# Initialize the model

model = TextGeneratorLSTM(vocab_size=5000,
embedding_dim=128, hidden_dim=512, output_dim=5000)
```

In this code:

- We define an LSTM-based text generator that predicts the next word in a sequence based on the input.

Text Generation with GPT-2

GPT-2 is a transformer model trained to generate coherent and realistic text. Here's how to use GPT-2 for text generation.

python

Copy code

```python
from transformers import GPT2LMHeadModel,
GPT2Tokenizer


# Load GPT-2 pre-trained model and tokenizer

tokenizer = GPT2Tokenizer.from_pretrained("gpt2")

model = GPT2LMHeadModel.from_pretrained("gpt2")


# Encode input text and generate output

input_text = "Once upon a time"
```

```python
input_ids = tokenizer.encode(input_text,
return_tensors="pt")


# Generate text from the input

generated_ids = model.generate(input_ids,
max_length=100, num_return_sequences=1)


# Decode and print the generated text

generated_text = tokenizer.decode(generated_ids[0],
skip_special_tokens=True)

print(generated_text)
```

In this example:

- We use the pre-trained GPT-2 model to generate text given a prompt.
- The generated text is a continuation of the input, showcasing GPT-2's text generation capabilities.

14.4. Building a Transformer-based Chatbot

A chatbot can be built using a transformer model like GPT-2 or BERT (for understanding user input). Here, we will build a simple transformer-based chatbot that generates responses to user queries.

python

Copy code

```python
from transformers import GPT2LMHeadModel,
GPT2Tokenizer


# Load GPT-2 model and tokenizer

tokenizer = GPT2Tokenizer.from_pretrained("gpt2")

model = GPT2LMHeadModel.from_pretrained("gpt2")


def generate_response(prompt):

    input_ids = tokenizer.encode(prompt,
return_tensors="pt")

    generated_ids = model.generate(input_ids,
max_length=50, num_return_sequences=1)

    response = tokenizer.decode(generated_ids[0],
skip_special_tokens=True)

    return response


# Test the chatbot

user_input = "Hello, how are you?"

print(generate_response(user_input))
```

In this code:

- We use GPT-2 to generate responses based on user input.
- The chatbot takes user input, encodes it, and uses the model to generate a response.

In this chapter, we explored various Natural Language Processing (NLP) tasks using LSTMs and Transformers:

- We covered sentiment analysis with LSTMs, demonstrating how to classify movie reviews as positive or negative.
- We discussed Named Entity Recognition (NER) using Transformers (BERT), enabling the identification of named entities in text.
- We demonstrated text generation with both LSTMs and GPT-2, showing how to generate text based on an input prompt.
- Finally, we built a transformer-based chatbot that generates conversational responses.

These techniques provide a solid foundation for building more complex NLP models and applications. In the next chapter, we will explore advanced transformer models and how to fine-tune them for specific tasks.

Chapter 15: Generative Models: Creating New Data

Generative models are a class of machine learning models designed to generate new, synthetic data that resembles a given dataset. These models can create entirely new images, text, music, and more, based on patterns learned from the input data. In this chapter, we will explore several types of generative models, including Generative Adversarial Networks (GANs) for image generation, Long Short-Term Memory (LSTM) networks for text generation, Convolutional Neural Networks (CNNs) for style transfer, and Recurrent Neural Networks (RNNs) for music generation.

We will dive into the following sections:

1. Image Generation with GANs (Faces, Art)
2. Text Generation with LSTMs
3. Style Transfer using CNNs
4. Music Generation using RNNs

15.1. Image Generation with GANs (Faces, Art)

Generative Adversarial Networks (GANs) are one of the most powerful tools for generating realistic images. GANs consist of two neural networks: the generator and the discriminator. The generator creates synthetic images, while the discriminator evaluates them, distinguishing between real and fake images. Through an adversarial process, the generator improves its ability to create realistic images as it tries to fool the discriminator.

The GAN Architecture

A GAN consists of two primary components:

1. Generator (G): Generates fake images from random noise (latent space).

2. Discriminator (D): Classifies images as real (from the dataset) or fake (from the generator).

The objective is for the generator to improve over time to generate images that the discriminator cannot distinguish from real images. The loss function for GANs involves both networks:

- Discriminator Loss: Measures how well the discriminator can differentiate between real and fake images.
- Generator Loss: Measures how well the generator can fool the discriminator.

Building a GAN for Image Generation (Faces, Art)

In this example, we will build a simple GAN to generate images. We will use a dataset such as CelebA (for faces) or Quick, Draw! (for artwork) to train the GAN.

Step 1: Define the Generator and Discriminator

python

Copy code

```python
import torch

import torch.nn as nn

import torch.optim as optim


# Define the generator
class Generator(nn.Module):

    def __init__(self):

        super(Generator, self).__init__()

        self.fc1 = nn.Linear(100, 256)
```

```python
        self.fc2 = nn.Linear(256, 512)

        self.fc3 = nn.Linear(512, 1024)

        self.fc4 = nn.Linear(1024, 28 * 28 * 1)  # Example for
MNIST (28x28 images)


    def forward(self, z):

        x = torch.relu(self.fc1(z))

        x = torch.relu(self.fc2(x))

        x = torch.relu(self.fc3(x))

        x = torch.tanh(self.fc4(x))

        return x.view(-1, 1, 28, 28)  # Reshape to image
dimensions


# Define the discriminator

class Discriminator(nn.Module):

    def __init__(self):

        super(Discriminator, self).__init__()

        self.fc1 = nn.Linear(28 * 28, 1024)

        self.fc2 = nn.Linear(1024, 512)

        self.fc3 = nn.Linear(512, 256)

        self.fc4 = nn.Linear(256, 1)
```

```python
def forward(self, x):

    x = x.view(-1, 28 * 28)  # Flatten the image

    x = torch.leaky_relu(self.fc1(x), 0.2)

    x = torch.leaky_relu(self.fc2(x), 0.2)

    x = torch.leaky_relu(self.fc3(x), 0.2)

    x = torch.sigmoid(self.fc4(x))  # Output probability

    return x
```

Step 2: Train the GAN

python

Copy code

```python
# Initialize the generator and discriminator

generator = Generator()

discriminator = Discriminator()


# Optimizers

lr = 0.0002

optimizer_g = optim.Adam(generator.parameters(), lr=lr, betas=(0.5, 0.999))

optimizer_d = optim.Adam(discriminator.parameters(), lr=lr, betas=(0.5, 0.999))
```

```python
# Loss function

criterion = nn.BCELoss()


# Training loop

for epoch in range(100):

    for real_images, _ in train_loader:  # Assume train_loader is the data loader

        # Train Discriminator

        optimizer_d.zero_grad()


        real_labels = torch.ones(batch_size, 1)

        fake_labels = torch.zeros(batch_size, 1)


        output = discriminator(real_images)

        loss_real = criterion(output, real_labels)


        z = torch.randn(batch_size, 100)  # Latent space (noise)

        fake_images = generator(z)

        output = discriminator(fake_images.detach())  # Detach to avoid gradients for fake images

        loss_fake = criterion(output, fake_labels)
```

```python
        loss_d = loss_real + loss_fake

        loss_d.backward()

        optimizer_d.step()


        # Train Generator

        optimizer_g.zero_grad()


        output = discriminator(fake_images)  # We want the
generator to fool the discriminator

        loss_g = criterion(output, real_labels)  # Fool the
discriminator into thinking fake images are real


        loss_g.backward()

        optimizer_g.step()


    print(f"Epoch [{epoch+1}/100], Loss D: {loss_d.item()},
Loss G: {loss_g.item()}")
```

In this code:

- We define a generator and a discriminator for the GAN model.
- The training loop alternates between updating the discriminator and the generator.

Results

After training the model, you should be able to generate realistic images resembling faces or artwork depending on the dataset used.

15.2. Text Generation with LSTMs

Text generation is a popular application of deep learning where the goal is to create new text that mimics the style or structure of a given dataset. LSTMs (Long Short-Term Memory networks) are well-suited for this task because they can capture long-range dependencies in sequences.

Building a Text Generator with LSTMs

For this example, we will use Shakespearean text as a dataset and generate new sentences in the style of Shakespeare.

Step 1: Prepare the Dataset

python

Copy code

```python
import torch

from torch.utils.data import Dataset, DataLoader


class TextDataset(Dataset):
    def __init__(self, text, seq_length):
        self.text = text
        self.seq_length = seq_length
        self.chars = sorted(list(set(text)))
```

```python
        self.char_to_idx = {ch: idx for idx, ch in
enumerate(self.chars)}

        self.idx_to_char = {idx: ch for idx, ch in
enumerate(self.chars)}


    def __len__(self):

        return len(self.text) - self.seq_length


    def __getitem__(self, idx):

        x = self.text[idx:idx + self.seq_length]

        y = self.text[idx + 1:idx + self.seq_length + 1]

        x_idx = torch.tensor([self.char_to_idx[ch] for ch in x],
dtype=torch.long)

        y_idx = torch.tensor([self.char_to_idx[ch] for ch in y],
dtype=torch.long)

        return x_idx, y_idx


# Load the text (e.g., Shakespeare's works)

with open("shakespeare.txt", "r") as file:

    text = file.read()


seq_length = 100

dataset = TextDataset(text, seq_length)
```

```python
dataloader = DataLoader(dataset, batch_size=64,
shuffle=True)
```

Step 2: Define the LSTM Model

python

Copy code

```python
class TextGeneratorLSTM(nn.Module):

    def __init__(self, vocab_size, hidden_dim, n_layers,
    seq_length):

        super(TextGeneratorLSTM, self).__init__()

        self.embedding = nn.Embedding(vocab_size,
        hidden_dim)

        self.lstm = nn.LSTM(hidden_dim, hidden_dim,
        num_layers=n_layers, batch_first=True)

        self.fc = nn.Linear(hidden_dim, vocab_size)

        self.seq_length = seq_length


    def forward(self, x):

        x = self.embedding(x)

        output, (hn, cn) = self.lstm(x)

        output = self.fc(output.reshape(-1, output.shape[2]))  #
        Reshape for classification

        return output
```

Step 3: Train the Model

python

Copy code

```python
model = TextGeneratorLSTM(vocab_size=len(dataset.chars), hidden_dim=256, n_layers=2, seq_length=seq_length)

optimizer = optim.Adam(model.parameters(), lr=0.002)

criterion = nn.CrossEntropyLoss()


for epoch in range(10):
    for x, y in dataloader:
        optimizer.zero_grad()
        output = model(x)
        loss = criterion(output, y.view(-1))
        loss.backward()
        optimizer.step()


    print(f"Epoch {epoch+1}, Loss: {loss.item()}")
```

In this code:

- We train an LSTM-based text generator on Shakespeare's works.
- The model learns to predict the next character in the sequence, and we use cross-entropy loss for training.

Step 4: Generate Text

python

Copy code

```python
def generate_text(model, start_string, length=200):

    model.eval()

    input_text = torch.tensor([dataset.char_to_idx[ch] for ch in start_string], dtype=torch.long).unsqueeze(0)

    hidden = None

    generated_text = start_string


    for _ in range(length):

        output, hidden = model(input_text)

        _, top_idx = torch.topk(output[-1], 1)

        next_char = dataset.idx_to_char[top_idx.item()]

        generated_text += next_char

        input_text = torch.tensor([top_idx.item()], dtype=torch.long).unsqueeze(0)


    return generated_text
```

```python
print(generate_text(model, "Shall I compare thee"))
```

This function generates text by repeatedly predicting the next character given a seed string.

15.3. Style Transfer using CNNs

Style transfer is a technique that allows you to apply the artistic style of one image to the content of another image. This is typically achieved using Convolutional Neural Networks (CNNs), particularly by minimizing a loss function that includes both content and style loss.

Step 1: Define the Loss Functions

python

Copy code

```python
import torch.nn.functional as F


def content_loss(content, target):

    return torch.mean((content - target) ** 2)


def style_loss(style, target):

    _, c, h, w = style.shape

    style_gram = gram_matrix(style)
```

```python
    target_gram = gram_matrix(target)

    return torch.mean((style_gram - target_gram) ** 2)


def gram_matrix(x):

    _, c, h, w = x.shape

    x = x.view(c, h * w)

    gram = torch.mm(x, x.t())

    return gram / (c * h * w)
```

Step 2: Apply Style Transfer

You can use a pre-trained CNN (e.g., VGG19) to extract content and style features from the images.

python

Copy code

```python
from torchvision import models


# Load a pre-trained VGG19 model

vgg = models.vgg19(pretrained=True).features.eval()


# Function to extract features

def extract_features(image, model):
```

```
layers = {'0': 'conv1_1', '5': 'conv2_1', '10': 'conv3_1', '19':
'conv4_1', '28': 'conv5_1'}

features = {}

x = image

for name, layer in model._modules.items():

    x = layer(x)

    if name in layers:

        features[layers[name]] = x

return features
```

Step 3: Train the Model

Apply style transfer by optimizing an image that minimizes both content and style losses.

15.4. Music Generation using RNNs

Music generation with Recurrent Neural Networks (RNNs) involves training a model on sequences of musical notes or audio features to generate new pieces of music. Here, we will explore a basic RNN architecture for generating music.

Step 1: Prepare the Dataset

The MAESTRO dataset is a collection of MIDI files, and we can use it for music generation tasks. You would preprocess the MIDI data into a sequence format for RNN input.

Step 2: Define the RNN Model

python

Copy code

```python
class MusicRNN(nn.Module):

    def __init__(self, input_size, hidden_size, output_size, n_layers=2):

        super(MusicRNN, self).__init__()

        self.rnn = nn.RNN(input_size, hidden_size, n_layers)

        self.fc = nn.Linear(hidden_size, output_size)


    def forward(self, x, hidden):

        rnn_out, hidden = self.rnn(x, hidden)

        output = self.fc(rnn_out)

        return output, hidden
```

Step 3: Train the RNN

python

Copy code

```python
model = MusicRNN(input_size=128, hidden_size=512, output_size=128)

optimizer = optim.Adam(model.parameters(), lr=0.001)

criterion = nn.CrossEntropyLoss()
```

Training loop would involve preparing input-output pairs and training the model similarly to text generation.

In this chapter, we explored the power of generative models in creating new data. We discussed the following topics:

- Image generation with GANs: How GANs can generate realistic images like faces or artwork.
- Text generation with LSTMs: How LSTMs can be used to generate text in the style of a particular author.
- Style transfer using CNNs: How CNNs can be used to transfer artistic styles from one image to another.
- Music generation using RNNs: How RNNs can generate new musical compositions based on patterns in training data.

These techniques open up exciting possibilities for creativity and automation in fields ranging from art and entertainment to content creation. In the next chapter, we will explore advanced generative models like VQ-VAE and Flow-based models.

Chapter 16: Reinforcement Learning in Games

Reinforcement Learning (RL) is a powerful branch of machine learning where agents learn to make decisions by interacting with an environment to maximize a reward signal. One of the most exciting applications of RL is in games, where agents can learn strategies, optimize their actions, and play at human or superhuman levels. In this chapter, we will explore how to train RL agents to play classic games like Atari games and Tic-Tac-Toe, introduce Deep Q-Learning(DQN) for game play, and demonstrate how to implement a self-playing agent using PyTorch.

16.1. Training Agents in Classic Games (Atari, Tic-Tac-Toe)

Training RL agents in classic games provides a great way to learn and implement core RL concepts. Two of the most famous examples are Atari games (such as Pong and Breakout) and simpler games like Tic-Tac-Toe.

Training Agents in Atari Games

Atari games are widely used for RL research because they provide a challenging environment where agents must learn to play from raw pixel data, often using deep neural networks. In 2013, DeepMind introduced Deep Q-Learning (DQN), which enabled an RL agent to learn Atari games directly from pixels and outperform human players on several games.

Step 1: Setting up the Atari Environment

We can use OpenAI's Gym to access Atari environments. OpenAI Gym provides a standard API for RL environments, including many Atari games.

bash

Copy code

```bash
pip install gym[atari]
```

python

Copy code

```python
import gym


# Create the Atari environment (Pong as an example)
env = gym.make("Pong-v0")


# Reset the environment to start a new episode
state = env.reset()


# Run a random agent to see the environment in action
for _ in range(1000):
    action = env.action_space.sample()  # Random action
    state, reward, done, info = env.step(action)
    env.render()  # Render the game screen
    if done:
        break
```

```
env.close()
```

In this example:

- We create an Atari environment (Pong-vo), which provides a state consisting of an image (the screen) and rewards that are used to evaluate the agent's performance.
- The agent takes random actions to interact with the game and the environment is rendered to visualize the game play.

Training an Agent in Tic-Tac-Toe

While Atari games are complex, simpler games like Tic-Tac-Toe can be a great starting point for understanding RL. In Tic-Tac-Toe, the agent must learn to play optimally by exploring actions in a small, discrete space.

Step 1: Setting up the Tic-Tac-Toe Environment

We define a simple Tic-Tac-Toe environment, where the agent will learn to play optimally.

python

Copy code

```python
import random


class TicTacToe:
    def __init__(self):
        self.board = [' '] * 9  # Empty board
        self.current_player = 'X'  # Player X starts
```

```python
    def reset(self):

        self.board = [' '] * 9

        self.current_player = 'X'

        return self.board


    def available_actions(self):

        return [i for i, x in enumerate(self.board) if x == ' ']


    def step(self, action):

        if self.board[action] != ' ':

            raise ValueError("Invalid action")

        self.board[action] = self.current_player

        if self.check_winner():

            return self.board, 1 if self.current_player == 'X' else -1, True

        elif all(x != ' ' for x in self.board):

            return self.board, 0, True  # Draw

        self.current_player = 'O' if self.current_player == 'X' else 'X'

        return self.board, 0, False
```

```python
def check_winner(self):
    # Check rows, columns, and diagonals for a winner
    win_conditions = [
        [0, 1, 2], [3, 4, 5], [6, 7, 8],  # Rows
        [0, 3, 6], [1, 4, 7], [2, 5, 8],  # Columns
        [0, 4, 8], [2, 4, 6]  # Diagonals
    ]
    for condition in win_conditions:
        if self.board[condition[0]] ==
self.board[condition[1]] == self.board[condition[2]] != ' ':
            return True
    return False


# Example of playing a random agent
env = TicTacToe()
state = env.reset()
done = False

while not done:
    action = random.choice(env.available_actions())  #
Random move
    state, reward, done = env.step(action)
```

```python
print(state)  # Print board after each move

print("Reward:", reward)
```

In this code:

- Tic-Tac-Toe is implemented with a board of 9 positions and two players (X and O).
- The agent makes random moves until the game ends. The step() function returns the new board state, the reward, and whether the game is over.

16.2. Deep Q-Learning for Game Play

Deep Q-Learning (DQN) is a popular RL algorithm where an agent learns to play games by approximating the Q-value function using a neural network. The Q-value represents the expected future reward for a given state-action pair.

Step 1: Define the Q-Network (Neural Network)

In DQN, we use a neural network to approximate the Q-values for all possible actions in a given state.

python

Copy code

```python
import torch

import torch.nn as nn

import torch.optim as optim

import numpy as np
```

```python
class QNetwork(nn.Module):

    def __init__(self, state_size, action_size):

        super(QNetwork, self).__init__()

        self.fc1 = nn.Linear(state_size, 64)

        self.fc2 = nn.Linear(64, 64)

        self.fc3 = nn.Linear(64, action_size)


    def forward(self, state):

        x = torch.relu(self.fc1(state))

        x = torch.relu(self.fc2(x))

        return self.fc3(x)


# Initialize the Q-Network

state_size = 4  # Example for a simple environment (e.g., Pong)

action_size = 2  # Example for a discrete action space (left or right)

q_network = QNetwork(state_size, action_size)


optimizer = optim.Adam(q_network.parameters(), lr=0.001)
```

Here, we define a simple feed-forward neural network with two hidden layers to approximate the Q-values for each action.

Step 2: Define the Experience Replay Buffer

Experience replay helps break the correlation between consecutive samples by storing past experiences and sampling from them randomly during training.

python

Copy code

```python
class ReplayBuffer:

    def __init__(self, capacity):

        self.buffer = []

        self.capacity = capacity


    def push(self, experience):

        self.buffer.append(experience)

        if len(self.buffer) > self.capacity:

            self.buffer.pop(0)


    def sample(self, batch_size):

        return random.sample(self.buffer, batch_size)
```

```python
def size(self):

    return len(self.buffer)
```

The replay buffer stores experiences in the form (state, action, reward, next_state).

Step 3: Q-Learning Update

In the Q-learning algorithm, we update the Q-values based on the Bellman equation.

python

Copy code

```python
def compute_td_loss(batch, q_network, target_network, gamma=0.99):

    states, actions, rewards, next_states, dones = zip(*batch)

    states = torch.tensor(states, dtype=torch.float32)

    actions = torch.tensor(actions, dtype=torch.long)

    rewards = torch.tensor(rewards, dtype=torch.float32)

    next_states = torch.tensor(next_states, dtype=torch.float32)

    dones = torch.tensor(dones, dtype=torch.bool)


    # Get Q values for the current state-action pairs

    q_values = q_network(states).gather(1, actions.unsqueeze(1))
```

```python
    # Get Q values for the next state (using target network for stability)
    next_q_values = target_network(next_states).max(1)[0]

    target_q_values = rewards + gamma * next_q_values * (~dones)


    # Compute loss
    loss = torch.mean((q_values - target_q_values.unsqueeze(1)) ** 2)

    return loss


# Example training loop
for epoch in range(1000):
    # Sample a batch of experiences
    batch = replay_buffer.sample(batch_size=64)

    loss = compute_td_loss(batch, q_network, target_network)

    optimizer.zero_grad()

    loss.backward()

    optimizer.step()
```

In this code:

- The loss function computes the Temporal Difference (TD) error based on the Q-value predictions and the target Q-values, which are computed using the Bellman equation.

16.3. Implementing a Self-Playing Agent with PyTorch

A self-playing agent is an agent that learns to play a game by interacting with itself. This type of agent is common in games like Chess, Go, and Atari games. Here, we will build a self-playing agent that learns by playing against itself, using the Q-learning algorithm and Deep Q-Networks.

Step 1: Set up the Self-Play Environment

In the case of games like Tic-Tac-Toe, the self-playing agent can interact with itself to generate training data.

python

Copy code

```python
class SelfPlayAgent:
    def __init__(self, model):
        self.model = model  # A Q-learning model

    def select_action(self, state, epsilon=0.1):
        if np.random.rand() < epsilon:
            return random.choice(env.available_actions())  # Explore
        else:
```

```python
        with torch.no_grad():

            q_values = self.model(state)

            return torch.argmax(q_values).item()  # Exploit


    def train(self, experience):

        self.model.train()

        optimizer.zero_grad()

        loss = compute_td_loss(experience, self.model,
self.target_network)

        loss.backward()

        optimizer.step()
```

Step 2: Training the Self-Playing Agent

The agent plays against itself, updating its knowledge after each episode.

python

Copy code

```python
agent = SelfPlayAgent(model)

for episode in range(10000):

    state = env.reset()

    done = False

    while not done:
```

```
action = agent.select_action(state)

next_state, reward, done = env.step(action)

agent.train((state, action, reward, next_state, done))

state = next_state
```

In this self-play loop:

- The agent plays by selecting actions based on the epsilon-greedy strategy (balancing exploration and exploitation).
- After each action, the agent learns by updating its Q-values.

In this chapter, we explored the application of Reinforcement Learning (RL) in games, covering:

- Training agents in classic games like Atari and Tic-Tac-Toe.
- The powerful Deep Q-Learning (DQN) algorithm, which enables agents to learn optimal strategies from high-dimensional inputs (like images).
- The process of building a self-playing agent that learns by interacting with itself, a concept widely used in competitive games.

These techniques enable agents to not only play games but also optimize their decision-making through trial and error, achieving optimal strategies. As we progress, these RL concepts can be applied to more complex environments, such as robotics, autonomous vehicles, and beyond.

Chapter 17: Industry Applications of Deep Learning

Deep learning has made significant strides in a variety of industries, providing powerful solutions to complex problems. From healthcare to autonomous vehicles, AI-driven technologies are transforming sectors by offering enhanced decision-making, automation, and efficiency. This chapter will explore four key industry applications of deep learning: Healthcare AI, Autonomous Vehicles, AI in Finance, and Natural Language Processing (NLP) for Customer Service and Chatbots. We will dive deep into each application, explaining the concepts, methods, and real-world examples.

17.1. Healthcare AI: Medical Image Classification (X-rays, MRI)

In healthcare, deep learning models have shown tremendous potential in assisting doctors and medical professionals by analyzing medical images to detect diseases and abnormalities. Medical image classification is one of the most popular applications of deep learning, particularly in the areas of radiology and oncology.

Medical Image Classification

Medical image classification uses deep learning models, particularly Convolutional Neural Networks (CNNs), to classify images into categories, such as detecting tumors in X-rays or MRI scans. These models are trained to recognize patterns in images and can be used to identify diseases such as cancer, pneumonia, or brain disorders.

Step 1: Data Preprocessing

Medical images are often complex and require preprocessing to make them suitable for training deep learning models. Common preprocessing steps include normalization, resizing, and augmentation.

python

Copy code

```python
import torch

import torchvision.transforms as transforms

from PIL import Image


# Example of preprocessing an image for a medical image classification model
transform = transforms.Compose([

    transforms.Resize((224, 224)),  # Resize the image

    transforms.Grayscale(num_output_channels=3),  # Convert to 3 channels if it's grayscale

    transforms.ToTensor(),  # Convert the image to a tensor

    transforms.Normalize(mean=[0.485, 0.456, 0.406], std=[0.229, 0.224, 0.225])  # Normalize

])


# Load an example X-ray image
img = Image.open("xray_example.png")

img = transform(img)

img = img.unsqueeze(0)  # Add batch dimension
```

In this example:

- The image is resized to fit the input size of a CNN (224x224 pixels).
- If the image is grayscale (common for X-rays), it is converted to a 3-channel format.
- The image is normalized with the mean and standard deviation of pre-trained models like ResNet.

Step 2: Model Training

In healthcare applications, CNNs have been shown to be highly effective. You can use pre-trained models like ResNet, VGG, or Inception for transfer learning. Here's an example of using a pre-trained ResNet for image classification:

python

Copy code

```python
import torch

import torch.nn as nn

import torchvision.models as models

import torch.optim as optim


# Load a pre-trained ResNet model

model = models.resnet18(pretrained=True)


# Modify the final layer for binary classification (e.g., disease vs no disease)
```

```python
model.fc = nn.Linear(model.fc.in_features, 2)


# Define the loss function and optimizer

criterion = nn.CrossEntropyLoss()

optimizer = optim.Adam(model.parameters(), lr=0.001)


# Train the model

model.train()

for epoch in range(10):

    optimizer.zero_grad()

    output = model(img)

    loss = criterion(output, torch.tensor([1]))  # Assuming label is 1 for diseased

    loss.backward()

    optimizer.step()

    print(f"Epoch [{epoch+1}/10], Loss: {loss.item()}")
```

In this code:

- ResNet-18 is used as a base model, pre-trained on ImageNet. The final layer is replaced to match the problem's output (e.g., binary classification).
- The model is trained for 10 epochs to classify the medical images into two categories.

Step 3: Model Evaluation

The performance of the model is evaluated using metrics like accuracy, precision, recall, and F1 score. For medical applications, high sensitivity (recall) is crucial to ensure that no potential cases are missed.

python

Copy code

```python
from sklearn.metrics import classification_report


# Example predictions (dummy values for illustration)

y_true = [1, 0, 1, 0, 1]

y_pred = [1, 0, 0, 0, 1]


# Print classification report

print(classification_report(y_true, y_pred))
```

A high recall ensures that the model is sensitive enough to detect diseases, which is essential in healthcare contexts where missing a diagnosis can have severe consequences.

17.2. Autonomous Vehicles: Object Detection and Navigation

Autonomous vehicles rely on deep learning models to navigate roads, detect objects, and make decisions in real-time. The primary tasks in autonomous driving are object detection, path planning, and navigation. Deep learning models, particularly CNNs and Recurrent Neural Networks (RNNs), are used to process sensor data (like camera images and LIDAR data) and guide the vehicle's actions.

Object Detection

Object detection is critical for identifying pedestrians, other vehicles, road signs, traffic lights, and obstacles. Deep learning models like YOLO (You Only Look Once) and Faster R-CNN are popular for real-time object detection tasks.

Step 1: Object Detection with YOLO

We can use a pre-trained YOLO model for detecting objects in images, such as cars or pedestrians.

python

Copy code

```python
import cv2

import torch

from torchvision import models, transforms


# Load pre-trained YOLOv3 model (or a similar object detection model)

model = models.detection.fasterrcnn_resnet50_fpn(pretrained=True)

model.eval()
```

```python
# Load an image (example of road image)

img = cv2.imread("road_image.jpg")

img = cv2.cvtColor(img, cv2.COLOR_BGR2RGB)


# Preprocess the image

transform = transforms.Compose([transforms.ToTensor()])

img_tensor = transform(img).unsqueeze(0)  # Add batch dimension


# Perform inference

with torch.no_grad():

    prediction = model(img_tensor)


# Get the predicted labels and bounding boxes

boxes = prediction[0]['boxes']

labels = prediction[0]['labels']

scores = prediction[0]['scores']
```

In this example:

- We use the Faster R-CNN model to perform object detection, detecting bounding boxes around objects in the image.

Step 2: Navigation and Path Planning

Once objects are detected, the next step is path planning, where the vehicle decides how to navigate based on the detected objects and road layout. Models like Deep Q-Learning and Proximal Policy Optimization (PPO) are used for training autonomous driving agents to make these decisions.

python

Copy code

```
# Example of Deep Q-Learning update for autonomous driving agent

# Assuming the environment is set up for driving

action_space = env.action_space.n  # Number of possible actions

state = env.reset()


# Define the Q-network (similar to previous DQN example)

q_network = QNetwork(state_size, action_space)

optimizer = optim.Adam(q_network.parameters(), lr=0.001)


# Training loop for DQN

for episode in range(100):

    state = env.reset()

    done = False
```

```
while not done:

    action = select_action(state)  # Select action using
epsilon-greedy policy

    next_state, reward, done, _ = env.step(action)


    # Store experience in replay buffer and train

    experience = (state, action, reward, next_state, done)

    replay_buffer.push(experience)

    train_dqn(q_network, optimizer, replay_buffer)

    state = next_state
```

In this code:

- The agent learns to take actions based on the environment's
  state, which includes real-time sensor data (camera, LIDAR)
  and the detected objects. The goal is to optimize the vehicle's
  navigation to avoid collisions and follow the road.

17.3. AI in Finance: Fraud Detection and Time-Series Forecasting

In finance, deep learning is used for a variety of tasks, including fraud
detection and time-series forecasting. These applications leverage
models to analyze financial data and make predictions, which can
improve decision-making and help prevent financial crimes.

Fraud Detection

Fraud detection involves identifying fraudulent transactions in a stream of financial data. Deep neural networks (DNNs)and autoencoders are often used to detect anomalies in transaction patterns.

Step 1: Anomaly Detection with Autoencoders

An autoencoder is trained to reconstruct the input data. If the reconstruction error is high, it indicates an anomaly, such as fraud.

python

Copy code

```python
import torch

import torch.nn as nn

import torch.optim as optim


# Define an autoencoder for anomaly detection
class Autoencoder(nn.Module):
    def __init__(self, input_dim):
        super(Autoencoder, self).__init__()
        self.encoder = nn.Linear(input_dim, 32)
        self.decoder = nn.Linear(32, input_dim)

    def forward(self, x):
        encoded = torch.relu(self.encoder(x))
        decoded = self.decoder(encoded)
```

```python
    return decoded

# Initialize the autoencoder

model = Autoencoder(input_dim=10)  # Example with 10
features per transaction


# Train the autoencoder

optimizer = optim.Adam(model.parameters(), lr=0.001)

criterion = nn.MSELoss()


# Example data (dummy values)

data = torch.randn(100, 10)  # 100 samples, 10 features
each

for epoch in range(100):

    optimizer.zero_grad()

    reconstructed = model(data)

    loss = criterion(reconstructed, data)

    loss.backward()

    optimizer.step()


    print(f"Epoch [{epoch+1}/100], Loss: {loss.item()}")
```

In this example:

- The autoencoder learns to reconstruct normal transaction data. High reconstruction error indicates an anomaly, which could be a fraudulent transaction.

Time-Series Forecasting

Deep learning models, particularly Recurrent Neural Networks (RNNs) and Long Short-Term Memory networks (LSTMs), are widely used for time-series forecasting. These models can predict stock prices, exchange rates, and other financial metrics based on historical data.

Step 1: Time-Series Forecasting with LSTMs

python

Copy code

```python
class TimeSeriesLSTM(nn.Module):

    def __init__(self, input_size, hidden_size, output_size):

        super(TimeSeriesLSTM, self).__init__()

        self.lstm = nn.LSTM(input_size, hidden_size, batch_first=True)

        self.fc = nn.Linear(hidden_size, output_size)


    def forward(self, x):

        lstm_out, _ = self.lstm(x)

        predictions = self.fc(lstm_out[:, -1, :])  # Use last LSTM output

        return predictions
```

```
# Example of forecasting

model = TimeSeriesLSTM(input_size=1, hidden_size=50,
output_size=1)
```

In this code:

- We use LSTM to predict future values in a time series. For example, the model can predict stock prices based on historical data.

17.4. Natural Language Processing for Customer Service and Chatbots

Natural Language Processing (NLP) plays a crucial role in automating customer service through chatbots, which can understand and respond to customer queries. Modern chatbots leverage advanced NLP techniques, including transformers and pre-trained models like BERT and GPT-3.

Step 1: Customer Query Classification

Customer queries often fall into different categories (e.g., billing issues, product inquiries). We can use NLP models to classify these queries.

python

Copy code

```
from transformers import BertTokenizer,
BertForSequenceClassification

import torch
```

```python
# Load pre-trained BERT model for text classification

model = BertForSequenceClassification.from_pretrained('bert-base-uncased', num_labels=3)  # Three classes

tokenizer = BertTokenizer.from_pretrained('bert-base-uncased')


# Tokenize input

inputs = tokenizer("How can I check my billing status?", return_tensors="pt")

outputs = model(**inputs)


# Get predicted class

predicted_class = torch.argmax(outputs.logits, dim=1)
```

In this example:

- BERT is used for classifying customer queries into categories (e.g., billing, support, general inquiries).

Step 2: Building a Chatbot

A chatbot can use transformers like GPT-3 to generate responses to customer queries.

python

Copy code

```python
from transformers import GPT2LMHeadModel,
GPT2Tokenizer


# Load GPT-2 model and tokenizer for generating responses

tokenizer = GPT2Tokenizer.from_pretrained("gpt2")

model = GPT2LMHeadModel.from_pretrained("gpt2")


def generate_response(prompt):

    input_ids = tokenizer.encode(prompt,
return_tensors="pt")

    outputs = model.generate(input_ids, max_length=100,
num_return_sequences=1)

    return tokenizer.decode(outputs[0],
skip_special_tokens=True)


# Example chatbot response

response = generate_response("How can I reset my
password?")

print(response)
```

This chatbot generates responses based on user inputs, providing a conversational experience for customer service.

In this chapter, we explored some of the most impactful deep learning applications in various industries:

- Healthcare AI: Medical image classification using CNNs to detect diseases from X-rays and MRIs.
- Autonomous Vehicles: Object detection and navigation systems for self-driving cars.
- AI in Finance: Fraud detection and time-series forecasting using neural networks.
- Natural Language Processing (NLP): Chatbots and customer service automation with transformers like GPT-3 and BERT.

These applications showcase the wide-ranging capabilities of deep learning in solving real-world problems across industries, from healthcare to finance and beyond. As deep learning continues to evolve, its applications are expected to grow and have an even greater impact on society.

Part 6

Appendices and Resources

Chapter 18: Appendices

In this chapter, we provide a collection of essential resources and guidance for working effectively with PyTorch. Whether you are a beginner or an experienced user, these tips and best practices will help you troubleshoot common issues, optimize model performance, explore advanced features, and convert PyTorch models to other frameworks like TensorFlow or Keras. This chapter is designed to be a comprehensive reference that complements the other chapters in the book.

18.1. PyTorch Best Practices

When working with PyTorch, adhering to best practices helps improve code quality, ensures model robustness, and facilitates easier debugging and maintenance. Below are some essential best practices for PyTorch development.

1. Organize Code into Modules

To enhance readability and maintainability, organize your code into modules. This includes:

- Model Definition: Keep your model architecture (layers, forward pass) in a separate Python class.
- Data Loading and Preprocessing: Define data transformations and loaders in a dedicated section.
- Training and Evaluation: Isolate training loops, evaluation, and inference in different functions.

Example:

python

Copy code

```
# model.py
```

```python
import torch.nn as nn


class SimpleNN(nn.Module):
    def __init__(self):
        super(SimpleNN, self).__init__()
        self.fc1 = nn.Linear(784, 128)
        self.fc2 = nn.Linear(128, 10)


    def forward(self, x):
        x = torch.relu(self.fc1(x))
        return self.fc2(x)


# data.py
from torch.utils.data import DataLoader, Dataset
from torchvision import transforms


class CustomDataset(Dataset):
    def __init__(self, data, labels, transform=None):
        self.data = data
        self.labels = labels
        self.transform = transform
```

```python
def __len__(self):
    return len(self.data)


def __getitem__(self, idx):
    sample = self.data[idx]
    label = self.labels[idx]
    if self.transform:
        sample = self.transform(sample)
    return sample, label
```

2. Use torch.device for Device Management

Explicitly managing computation devices (CPU or GPU) ensures that the model and data are moved to the appropriate device before training or evaluation.

python

Copy code

```python
device = torch.device("cuda" if torch.cuda.is_available() else "cpu")

model = SimpleNN().to(device)  # Move model to the GPU (if available)

inputs, labels = inputs.to(device), labels.to(device)  # Move data to device
```

3. Model Initialization

Proper initialization of model weights can significantly impact training convergence. PyTorch's torch.nn.init module provides various initialization methods (e.g., Xavier, He).

python

Copy code

```python
import torch.nn.init as init


def init_weights(m):

    if isinstance(m, nn.Linear):

        init.kaiming_normal_(m.weight, mode='fan_out',
nonlinearity='relu')

        if m.bias is not None:

            init.constant_(m.bias, 0)


model.apply(init_weights)  # Apply weight initialization to
all layers
```

4. Use torch.optim for Optimizers

PyTorch provides several built-in optimizers (e.g., SGD, Adam). You should always use torch.optim for managing the model's parameters.

python

Copy code

```
optimizer = torch.optim.Adam(model.parameters(),
lr=0.001)
```

5. Saving and Loading Models

Saving and loading models using torch.save and torch.load is essential for preserving trained models and continuing from saved checkpoints.

python

Copy code

```
# Save model

torch.save(model.state_dict(), 'model.pth')


# Load model

model = SimpleNN()

model.load_state_dict(torch.load('model.pth'))

model.eval()
```

18.2. Troubleshooting Common Issues in PyTorch

Even with PyTorch's user-friendly interface, issues can arise during model training, data loading, and evaluation. Below are some common problems and solutions.

1. CUDA Out of Memory

Error: RuntimeError: CUDA out of memory.

Solution:

- Reduce the batch size.
- Use torch.no_grad() during evaluation or inference to avoid unnecessary gradient computations.
- Clear GPU memory manually using torch.cuda.empty_cache().

python

Copy code

```
torch.cuda.empty_cache()  # Clears the cache
```

2. Mismatched Dimensions

Error: RuntimeError: size mismatch, m1: ...

Solution:

- Verify that input tensors are properly shaped before feeding them into the model.
- For convolutional layers, ensure the image size is compatible with the network's input size.
- Use print(input_tensor.shape) for debugging tensor dimensions.

3. NaN Loss During Training

Error: NaN values encountered in loss function.

Solution:

- Check the learning rate: a large learning rate can cause instability.
- Add gradient clipping to prevent exploding gradients.

python

Copy code

```
torch.nn.utils.clip_grad_norm_(model.parameters(),
max_norm=1.0)
```

4. Unused Variables Warning

Error: UserWarning: This variable is not used by any gradient computation.

Solution:

- Ensure that all operations contributing to the loss are properly connected to the computation graph.
- Avoid manually modifying the graph, which may disconnect parts of the model.

18.3. Performance Optimization Tips

Efficient training and inference are essential for deploying deep learning models in production environments. Below are some performance optimization tips:

1. Utilize GPU Acceleration

Ensure your model and data are transferred to the GPU for training.

python

Copy code

```
device = torch.device("cuda" if torch.cuda.is_available()
else "cpu")
```

```python
model = model.to(device)

inputs, labels = inputs.to(device), labels.to(device)
```

2. Use Mixed Precision Training

Mixed precision training leverages 16-bit floating-point precision to speed up training and reduce memory usage while maintaining model accuracy.

python

Copy code

```python
from torch.cuda.amp import autocast, GradScaler


scaler = GradScaler()


for data, target in train_loader:
    optimizer.zero_grad()
    with autocast():  # Automatically use mixed precision
        output = model(data)
        loss = criterion(output, target)
    scaler.scale(loss).backward()
    scaler.step(optimizer)
    scaler.update()
```

3. Use Data Parallelism

For multi-GPU setups, use torch.nn.DataParallel or torch.distributed for parallel training across multiple GPUs.

python

Copy code

```
model = nn.DataParallel(model)

model = model.to(device)
```

4. Efficient Data Loading

Use DataLoader with appropriate num_workers to speed up data loading.

python

Copy code

```
train_loader = DataLoader(dataset, batch_size=64,
num_workers=4, shuffle=True)
```

5. Profiling and Debugging

Use PyTorch Profiler for identifying performance bottlenecks.

python

Copy code

```
import torch.profiler
```

```python
with torch.profiler.profile(with_stack=True) as prof:

    model(input_tensor)


print(prof.key_averages().table(sort_by="cpu_time_total")
)
```

18.4. Advanced PyTorch Features

Creating custom layers is a common requirement for advanced architectures. PyTorch allows users to create their own layers by subclassing nn.Module.

python

Copy code

```python
class CustomLayer(nn.Module):

    def __init__(self):

        super(CustomLayer, self).__init__()

        self.conv = nn.Conv2d(3, 64, kernel_size=3, padding=1)

        self.fc = nn.Linear(64, 10)


    def forward(self, x):

        x = self.conv(x)

        x = torch.relu(x)
```

```python
    x = torch.flatten(x, 1)

    x = self.fc(x)

    return x


# Use the custom layer in a model

model = CustomLayer()
```

PyTorch hooks are functions that can be attached to tensors, modules, or gradients to capture intermediate outputs, gradients, or modify them during the forward or backward pass.

python

Copy code

```python
# Example of registering a hook to capture gradients

def print_grad(grad):

    print("Gradient:", grad)


# Register hook to the first layer of a model

hook = model.conv.register_backward_hook(print_grad)


# During backpropagation, the gradient of the first
# convolutional layer will be printed

output = model(input_tensor)
```

```
output.backward()
```

18.5. Converting PyTorch Models to Other Frameworks (TensorFlow, Keras)

Sometimes, you may need to convert a PyTorch model to another framework like TensorFlow or Keras for deployment purposes. PyTorch provides tools to facilitate this process.

1. Using ONNX for Model Conversion

ONNX (Open Neural Network Exchange) is an open format for representing machine learning models. You can export your PyTorch model to ONNX and import it into other frameworks like TensorFlow.

python

Copy code

```python
import torch.onnx


# Export PyTorch model to ONNX

dummy_input = torch.randn(1, 3, 224, 224)

torch.onnx.export(model, dummy_input, "model.onnx")


# Load ONNX model in TensorFlow or other frameworks

# For TensorFlow, you can use the ONNX-TensorFlow converter
```

2. Using tf-pytorch for Direct Conversion

tf-pytorch is a library that allows converting PyTorch models directly to TensorFlow/Keras models.

bash

Copy code

```bash
pip install tf-pytorch
```

python

Copy code

```python
from tf_pytorch import convert

# Convert PyTorch model to Keras model

keras_model = convert(pytorch_model)
```

This tool helps seamlessly convert between PyTorch and Keras models while preserving model weights and architecture.

This chapter provided a set of tools, tips, and best practices for working with PyTorch. We covered essential aspects like:

- PyTorch best practices for organizing code and handling devices.
- Troubleshooting common issues such as CUDA memory errors and NaN loss values.
- Performance optimization techniques, including mixed precision training and parallelism.

- Advanced features such as creating custom layers and using hooks for model introspection.
- The process of converting PyTorch models to other frameworks using ONNX or direct conversion tools like tf-pytorch.

By following these practices and using the provided tools, you can build more efficient, maintainable, and scalable deep learning models in PyTorch.

Chapter 19: Resources and Further Reading

As you progress in your deep learning journey with PyTorch, having access to quality resources and further reading material is essential. This chapter provides you with a comprehensive list of recommended books, papers, tutorials, courses, libraries, and GitHub repositories to deepen your knowledge and expand your skills in deep learning. These resources will help you stay up to date with the latest advancements, find solutions to challenges, and explore more specialized topics in the field of AI.

19.1. Recommended Books, Papers, and Articles

The following books, research papers, and articles are essential reads for anyone serious about mastering deep learning and PyTorch. They cover foundational concepts, state-of-the-art techniques, and practical applications.

Books

1. "Deep Learning" by Ian Goodfellow, Yoshua Bengio, and Aaron Courville
   This book is a must-read for anyone interested in deep learning. It provides a comprehensive and rigorous introduction to the field, covering everything from the basics of neural networks to advanced techniques such as convolutional and recurrent networks, deep reinforcement learning, and unsupervised learning. It's the foundational text for deep learning theory.
2. "Deep Learning with PyTorch" by Eli Stevens, Luca Antiga, and Thomas Viehmann
   This book focuses on practical deep learning with PyTorch. It covers all the necessary concepts to use PyTorch effectively, including how to build models, optimize them, and deploy

them for real-world tasks. It's perfect for practitioners who want a hands-on guide to PyTorch.

3. "Hands-On Machine Learning with Scikit-Learn, Keras, and TensorFlow" by Aurélien Géron
   This book provides a practical approach to machine learning, including deep learning. While it mainly uses TensorFlow, it provides important insights into how machine learning models work and offers practical advice on building and deploying models.

4. "Neural Networks and Deep Learning" by Michael Nielsen
   A fantastic online book that gives a clear and intuitive introduction to neural networks and deep learning. It explains the core ideas behind backpropagation, gradient descent, and deep networks, and is ideal for beginners.

5. "Deep Reinforcement Learning Hands-On" by Maxim Lapan
   This book focuses on reinforcement learning (RL) with deep learning, offering hands-on examples and implementations using PyTorch. It's perfect for those interested in developing RL models for real-world applications.

Papers

1. "Attention is All You Need" by Vaswani et al. (2017)
   This groundbreaking paper introduces the Transformer architecture, which has revolutionized NLP and other sequential tasks. It's essential for understanding the self-attention mechanism used in modern models like BERT and GPT-3.

2. "Mastering Chess and Shogi by Self-Play with a General Reinforcement Learning Algorithm" by Silver et al. (2017)
   This paper details the development of AlphaZero, which uses deep reinforcement learning to master chess and shogi without prior knowledge. The algorithms and techniques discussed are cutting-edge and widely applicable to other games and domains.

3. "ImageNet Large Scale Visual Recognition Challenge" by Russakovsky et al. (2015)

The ImageNet challenge was a pivotal moment in deep learning history. This paper discusses the results of the ImageNet competition and the architectures that led to breakthroughs in computer vision.

4. "Generative Adversarial Nets" by Goodfellow et al. (2014)
   This paper introduces Generative Adversarial Networks (GANs), a powerful method for generating realistic synthetic data. It is a foundational read for anyone working with generative models.

Articles

1. "A Beginner's Guide to Neural Networks and Deep Learning" by Skymind
   This article provides a high-level overview of neural networks and deep learning, designed for beginners. It's a good starting point for understanding how neural networks work.

2. "PyTorch 101: A Guide to Getting Started with Deep Learning" by PyTorch.org
   PyTorch's official blog provides helpful guides, tutorials, and case studies that demonstrate how to get started with deep learning using PyTorch. It's a valuable resource for beginners and intermediates.

19.2. PyTorch Documentation and Tutorials

The official PyTorch documentation is the best place to explore the PyTorch framework, as it is continuously updated with the latest changes and improvements. The following resources will help you navigate through PyTorch's core concepts and advanced features.

1. PyTorch Documentation
   The official PyTorch documentation is comprehensive and covers everything from basic tensor operations to advanced topics like distributed training, custom layers, and deployment.

It includes code snippets, explanations, and examples for each component of the library.

2. PyTorch Tutorials

   The PyTorch Tutorials page offers a range of tutorials, from introductory content to more advanced topics such as reinforcement learning, transfer learning, and deployment. Some recommended tutorials include:

   - "PyTorch for Deep Learning": A detailed series of tutorials covering everything from tensors and autograd to CNNs, RNNs, and GANs.
   - "Transfer Learning with PyTorch": Learn how to use pre-trained models for new tasks, significantly reducing training time and computational cost.
   - "TorchScript and Model Deployment": This tutorial explains how to export models to TorchScript and deploy them in production environments.

3. PyTorch Lightning Documentation

   PyTorch Lightning is a popular library that simplifies PyTorch code by abstracting away boilerplate code and improving scalability. The official documentation provides clear guidelines for leveraging this high-level framework in your projects.

19.3. Online Courses and Communities

Deep learning is a rapidly evolving field, and staying up to date requires continuous learning. The following online courses and communities provide excellent opportunities for hands-on learning and engaging with other PyTorch enthusiasts.

Online Courses

1. "Deep Learning Specialization" by Andrew Ng (Coursera)
   This specialization offers a structured introduction to deep learning, covering CNNs, RNNs, and more. Although it

primarily uses TensorFlow, the concepts taught are directly applicable to PyTorch.

2. "Fast.ai Deep Learning for Coders"
   Fast.ai provides a highly practical deep learning course that uses PyTorch as its primary framework. The course emphasizes creating deep learning models quickly and effectively, and it's suitable for both beginners and experienced developers.

3. "PyTorch Fundamentals" by Udacity
   This free course by Udacity teaches the fundamentals of deep learning using PyTorch, including building neural networks, training models, and working with real-world datasets.

4. "CS231n: Convolutional Neural Networks for Visual Recognition" by Stanford University
   This is one of the best courses for understanding computer vision and deep learning. The course uses both PyTorch and TensorFlow for hands-on projects and assignments.

Communities

1. PyTorch Discussion Forum
   The PyTorch Discussion Forum is an active community where users share solutions, ask questions, and help others with PyTorch issues. It's a great place to get support and connect with the PyTorch community.

2. Stack Overflow
   Stack Overflow has a large number of questions and answers related to PyTorch. You can find solutions to common problems or post your own questions with the pytorch tag.

3. Reddit
   The PyTorch subreddit is another active community where users discuss news, research, and issues related to PyTorch. It's an excellent resource for staying up to date and finding inspiration.

19.4. Useful Libraries and Frameworks for Deep Learning

While PyTorch is powerful on its own, several libraries and frameworks can be used alongside it to enhance functionality, streamline workflows, and integrate with other technologies.

1. PyTorch Lightning

PyTorch Lightning is a lightweight framework built on top of PyTorch that abstracts away much of the boilerplate code needed for training models. It helps you write cleaner, more scalable, and reproducible code.

- Key Features: Simplified model training, multi-GPU support, model checkpoints, distributed training.

2. Hugging Face Transformers

The Hugging Face Transformers library provides pre-trained models and easy-to-use interfaces for a wide range of natural language processing tasks, such as text classification, translation, summarization, and question answering.

- Key Features: State-of-the-art transformer models (BERT, GPT-2, T5), easy integration with PyTorch, and fine-tuning pre-trained models.

3. TensorBoardX

TensorBoardX is a PyTorch-compatible tool that allows you to visualize training metrics (like loss curves, gradients, and model graphs) in real-time, using the popular TensorBoard interface.

- Key Features: Visualizations for training metrics, hyperparameter tuning, model graph visualization.

4. ONNX (Open Neural Network Exchange)

ONNX is an open format for representing machine learning models that allows interoperability between different frameworks like PyTorch and TensorFlow. You can use ONNX to export PyTorch models and run them in other frameworks or deploy them to production.

- Key Features: Model interoperability, support for a wide range of ML frameworks, deployment flexibility.

19.5. GitHub Repositories for PyTorch Projects

GitHub is the hub for open-source projects, and there are numerous high-quality PyTorch repositories that provide implementations of models, tutorials, and research papers. Here are some valuable repositories to explore:

1. PyTorch Examples

The PyTorch Examples repository contains implementations of common deep learning models like CNNs, RNNs, GANs, and reinforcement learning algorithms. It's a great place to explore practical PyTorch code.

2. Fastai

The Fastai GitHub repository provides tools for deep learning and includes a set of high-level APIs that make it easier to experiment with PyTorch.

3. Hugging Face Transformers

The Hugging Face Transformers repository contains state-of-the-art models for natural language processing, including BERT, GPT-2, T5, and more.

4. PyTorch Geometric

PyTorch Geometric is a library that specializes in deep learning on graphs and geometric data. It includes implementations of graph neural networks (GNNs) and related algorithms.

In this chapter, we've compiled a comprehensive set of resources that will help you continue your journey with PyTorchand deep learning. Whether you're looking to deepen your understanding of core concepts through books and papers, enhance your skills with courses and communities, or improve your workflows with useful libraries, these resources will equip you with the tools you need to succeed.

Deep learning is a fast-moving field, and staying up to date with the latest research, techniques, and libraries is crucial for advancing your knowledge and skills. Keep exploring and experimenting, and you'll be well on your way to mastering deep learning with PyTorch!

Index

An index is a critical tool for a well-organized and navigable book, especially for technical topics like deep learning and PyTorch. It helps readers quickly locate specific information, concepts, and examples within the book. In this chapter, we will outline how to create an effective index for your book, "Hands-On Deep Learning with PyTorch: From Fundamentals to Advanced Projects", ensuring that it's detailed, clear, and user-friendly.

Key Principles for an Effective Index

1. Comprehensiveness: The index should cover all the important concepts, techniques, and tools discussed in the book.
2. Organization: Entries should be organized alphabetically, and related concepts should be grouped together for easy navigation.
3. Clarity: Use clear, concise terms in the index entries so that readers can understand at a glance what they will find.
4. Cross-Referencing: Where relevant, cross-references should be used to guide readers to related content elsewhere in the book.
5. Consistency: The same terms should be indexed in the same manner throughout the book, avoiding confusion.

How to Structure the Index

The index will generally consist of the following elements:

- Main Entries: These are the primary concepts, terms, or sections of the book that the reader might be searching for.
- Subentries: These are more specific topics or detailed concepts related to the main entry.
- Page Numbers: Each entry should list the relevant pages where the concept is discussed in the book.

Creating the Index for "Hands-On Deep Learning with PyTorch"

Here's an example of what the index might look like for key topics covered in the book. I will include main entries, subentries, and related references that could help users find information quickly.

A

B

C

- ○ Fine-tuning pre-trained models, 146
- Training loops, 90
  - ○ Epochs and batches, 91

Cross-References

Throughout the index, we use cross-references to guide readers to related topics. For example:

- Model evaluation, 106, see also Loss functions, 107
- Deep Q-Learning, 175, see also Reinforcement learning, 170

This helps readers easily navigate between related topics without having to search for them individually.

Creating the Index: Best Practices

1. Start Early: It's easier to create an index as you write the book, adding entries while drafting each chapter, rather than attempting to create it afterward.
2. Be Consistent: Use consistent terms and phrasing for indexing, such as referring to "activation functions" and not switching between "activation" and "activations."
3. Include Synonyms: Readers may search for a concept by using synonyms, so include variations of terms (e.g., "Convolutional Neural Networks" and "CNNs").
4. Avoid Overloading: While being thorough is essential, an overly long list of subentries for each main topic can be overwhelming. Prioritize key concepts and high-importance references.
5. Include Examples: Where applicable, include specific examples in the index for terms like "training loop" or "image augmentation" to guide the reader directly to the correct sections.

An effective index is an invaluable tool that enhances the usability and accessibility of your book. By following the guidelines and example outlined here, you can create a detailed, well-organized, and easy-to-navigate index that will help readers quickly find the information they need. A well-crafted index not only improves the reading experience but also ensures that your deep learning content in PyTorch is efficiently organized for future reference.